Read-Alouds
With Young Children

Robin Campbell

University of Hertfordshire
Watford, United Kingdom

INTERNATIONAL
Reading
Association
800 Barksdale Road, PO Box 8139
Newark, Delaware 19714-8139, USA
www.reading.org

The International Reading Association attempts, through its publications, to provide a forum for a wide spectrum of opinions on reading. This policy permits divergent viewpoints without implying the endorsement of the Association.

Director of Publications   Joan M. Irwin
Editorial Director, Books and Special Projects   Matthew W. Baker
Special Projects Editor   Tori Mello Bachman
Permissions Editor   Janet S. Parrack
Associate Editor   Jeanine K. McGann
Production Editor   Shannon Benner
Editorial Assistant   Tyanna L. Collins
Publications Manager   Beth Doughty
Production Department Manager   Iona Sauscermen
Art Director   Boni Nash
Supervisor, Electronic Publishing   Anette Schütz-Ruff
Senior Electronic Publishing Specialist   Cheryl J. Strum
Electronic Publishing Specialist   Lynn Harrison
Proofreader   Charlene Nichols

Photo Credits   Cover design: Judi Connelly
                     Cover photo: Jonathan A. Meyers

Library of Congress Cataloging in Publication Data
Campbell, Robin, 1937–
    Read-alouds with young children / Robin Campbell.
        p.   cm.
    Includes bibliographical references.
    ISBN 0-87207-289-4
    1. Reading (Early childhood)   2. Oral reading.   3. Language arts (Early childhood)   4. Children—Books and reading.   I. Title.
    LB1139.5.R43 C27   2001   2001000630
    372.4—dc21

Second Printing, September 2001

Contents

Introduction

In the United States, the term *read-aloud* describes the worldwide phenomenon of an adult reading a book to a young child or a group of children (Trelease, 1995). In New Zealand the same practice has been referred to as *storybook reading* (Phillips & McNaughton, 1990); in the United Kingdom it's simply called *story reading* (Campbell, 1990). *Read-Alouds With Young Children* explores read-alouds in both home and school settings with young children. In the United States, this includes children in kindergarten through third grade. In England, the site of many of the classrooms I observed for this book, those early years include nursery or preschool classrooms at 3 and 4 years of age, the reception (kindergarten) class of a primary school at 5 years of age, and years 1 and 2 (or grades 1 and 2) at 6 and 7 years of age. For both preprimary and primary children, the British national curriculum suggests the use of story readings or read-alouds to encourage literacy learning. A read-aloud can stand alone, but *Read-Alouds With Young Children* focuses on activities that can stem from this practice. Teachers of young children, and teacher educators, are likely to find this book useful as a means of reconsidering read-alouds and their contribution to a literacy curriculum. Parents too will be interested to note how their read-alouds at home provide a foundation for children's reading and writing development.

As Susan Neuman (1998) notes, during read-alouds the teacher often will engage the children to respond in a variety of ways to the story that has been read. The interactive read-aloud is an important literacy activity that is recognized as a developmentally appropriate practice for young children (International Reading Association & National Association for the Education of Young Children, 1998). Support for the activity includes research evidence from projects exploring literacy development at home, and explorations of read-alouds in school settings.

Literacy Development at Home

The longitudinal Children Learning to Read Project in Bristol, England, directed by Gordon Wells, is one of the most frequently cited

1

projects on this topic. In this study, children were observed from shortly after their first birthday until they were 10 years old. It was found that those children who demonstrated a relatively high understanding of print as they started school at age 5 were more likely to achieve high levels of reading at age 10. But how was that understanding of print acquired? The researchers found that the parents' read-alouds had a positive influence on the literacy development of their children, and that the children's experience listening to stories significantly related to their understanding of print (Wells, 1986). In addition, the opportunities for children to watch the parent handle the book and to be involved in discussions about the story were all valuable parts of the read-aloud.

Shirley Brice Heath (1983) confirms the value of parent-child read-alouds for preschool children and the importance of the interactive experience. She studied three neighboring communities in the United States and considered the literacy experiences of preschool children. Each of the communities demonstrated different adult practices, which led to different outcomes for the children at school. In one community, the parents read storybooks to their children and did so interactively. As we would now expect, children in that environment were successful at reading in school. In another community, the parents read to their children and helped them with letter names, but the readings were not interactive; there was no encouragement for the children to be involved in the story readings. The children did well initially at school and managed such tasks as completing workbook pages, but they were less successful in the later elementary grades. The children in the third community were least successful at reading in school. Although the parents valued school for the benefits it might bring to their children, they did not provide the same learning environment at home. Story readings were largely absent from the children's preschool experiences.

Work by Denny Taylor and Dorothy Strickland (1986) also discusses the benefits of family storybook readings, but is quite different in its approach. The authors provide numerous excerpts from parent-child read-alouds, and there are many illustrations that demonstrate the intensity of the children's involvement. The read-alouds from many different homes are used to demonstrate the learning that takes place beyond the story itself. The authors show how the children learned a sense of how stories are constructed, and how that helped them understand other stories and create their own. The children also extended their vocabulary as they interacted with a parent during the story readings. Not only did they learn individual words, but they also were introduced to language patterns that are contained in stories, and they began to play with the sounds of language. The read-aloud experience also reinforced the importance of the listening skills the children later used to support their classroom learning.

Although the Taylor and Strickland book is extensively about storybook readings, it also links with a main theme of *Read-Alouds With Young Children*: Read-alouds can provide the basis for other activities. Their findings show that stories that are read aloud provide an interest and stimulus for children and parents to create their own books. Therefore, the authors suggest that the children should have a thick pad of plain paper and a box of crayons or felt pens to make their own response to the stories. These responses can lead to parents and children working together to make their own family storybooks. In the authors' work, one child extends her interest in cats to create her own storybook about them; this example demonstrates how children use their experiences to draw and write with feeling (pp. 75–76).

Although it is not practical to discuss all the studies that support the benefits of story reading at home, I will recognize one voice of dissent. Scarborough and Dobrich (1994) reviewed a large number of correlation studies and argue that the extent of the relation between parent-preschooler reading and subsequent literacy achievement was less than is usually claimed. The responses to that article were immediate: Lonigan (1994) presents a more optimistic view of the data analyzed, and Dunning, Mason, and Stewart (1994) suggest that the data indicate that story reading does have an important influence on children's developing literacy and is a literacy activity that warrants further attention. It is important to note that the data explored in this debate did not include the rich and detailed accounts of individual preschool children enjoying read-alouds.

Children Developing as Literacy Users

A number of longitudinal studies of individual children add to our understanding of the importance of read-alouds. These studies typically follow children in their first 5 years of life. In many cases the researchers were studying their own children, but because these studies are numerous, we can begin to look objectively at the data they provide. One of the best known studies is that of Glenda Bissex (1980). Bissex read stories to her son Paul before he started to talk; those read-alouds enabled Paul to recognize stories and provide an emergent reading before he turned 3.

Judith Schickedanz (1990) reports on the development of her son Adam's writing, indicating that Adam sought repeated readings of favorite books from about 16 months until the age of 3 years. After that his preference was for information-rich nonfiction books. In other studies by parents of young children (Baghban, 1984; Laminack, 1991; Martens, 1996) there is evidence that suggests that read-alouds are an important contributor to a child's literacy development. Baghban includes transcripts to show how her daughter Giti developed as a reader between 30 and 33 months as she returned frequently to previously read texts.

A few studies have concentrated more exclusively on the interactions between parents and children during read-alouds. Jones (1996) was unusual in that she limited her study to the first 2 years. However, she did note the physical, mental, and emotional pleasures of read-alouds. Spreadbury (1994) and Doake (1988) followed children for a longer period of time, and both indicated that story readings were an important feature supporting literacy development. Doake concluded that "children who are read to regularly by their parents and teachers are being given what they are entitled to in a society that expects them to become fully literate" (p. 48).

In addition, there are two studies (Campbell, 1999; White, 1954/1984) that specifically record a child's development in conjunction with read-alouds. Dorothy White, a children's librarian, shared a wide variety of books with her daughter Carol between the ages of 2 and 5. White's study presents a diary of those shared readings and demonstrates the enormous enjoyment that came from the readings and the influence of the books on Carol's language and play. In *Literacy From Home to School: Reading With Alice* (Campbell, 1999), I report on how my granddaughter Alice also listened to stories on a daily basis, including many repeated readings of favorite books. My study includes transcripts of Alice's involvement in the story readings and shows her progress as a reader from birth to 5 years of age. She made a contribution to the reading of a short book when she was almost 2. Then she extended those contributions with other books until she memorized whole stories. That memorization enabled her to begin to see links with the print, and at 3 years, 9 months, she made known that attention to print when sharing *Zoo Animals* (Butterfield, 1995):

Alice:	Look there's *and* and *zoo*.
Grandfather:	Yes, that says *and* and that word is *zoo*. It's a book about zoo animals, isn't it?
Alice:	Mmh, I like the hippo best.
Grandfather:	That hippo gets all muddy, doesn't it? (Campbell, 1999, p. 86).

Alice's recognition of some print enabled her to begin to read from previously shared books. Then all those events contributed to her willingness to read short unfamiliar books by the time she was 5 years old. Story readings with adults were a key feature supporting that development.

Read-Alouds in School

Do read-alouds work in a similarly effective way in school? A frequently cited study of school read-alouds is that of Feitelson, Kita, and Goldstein (1986). The authors followed two teachers who were working with first-grade classes as they read to the children for 20 minutes at the end of the school day. One of the teachers believed that the reading consumed too much time, so she stopped those daily readings. When given reading tests at the end of the study, the children in the class that continued with read-alouds performed better.

Smith and Elley (1994) briefly review the outcomes of some of the research dealing with read-alouds. That includes some earlier work by Elley (1989) that demonstrates vocabulary gains among 8- and 9-year-old children from the stories that were read to them. The gains were extended when the teacher explained or illustrated the target words. Morrow (1992) also notes literacy gains among children from minority backgrounds when a literature-based program was developed with second-grade children. An important part of the program was the daily read-aloud and the activities that were developed from those read-alouds.

Learning From Read-Alouds

It is difficult to isolate the literacy gains that accrue from read-alouds, but the activity does appear to provide many benefits for young children. Marriott (1995) indicates very boldly that "it is almost impossible to overemphasize the value of this activity for children of any age or reading level" (p. 65).

Story read-alouds provide the basis for children to learn about literacy, to become readers and writers, to learn through literacy, and to want to read in the future (Sloan, 1991). At the same time, writers such as Money (1987) remind us that teachers should ensure that the child's response to and enjoyment of the story or poem itself remains paramount.

Children arrive at preschool or kindergarten with a wide range of differing experiences of books. Some children have had the joy of hearing hundreds of stories read to and with them. And because stories are often read aloud more than once, these children may have experienced thousands of story readings in total. If the teacher continues with those read-alouds and the repeat readings of a story, then these children have a link between home and school. They are immediately able to extend and develop their literacy learning because they are in the familiar territory of narrative with interesting characters, stimulating events, and thought-provoking outcomes.

Children without the experience of read-alouds at home benefit from having frequent and regular story readings in their classroom. They need to explore the delights of storybooks with the support of adults who read to them and discuss aspects of the stories. As Moustafa (1997) argues,

> The primary literacy education task of preschool and early school years is not teaching children letter-sound correspondences but reading to them. Reading to children in school should be a daily activity, as important a part of a child's class schedule as math and lunch. If a child is experiencing difficulty in learning to read, we should not ask if he or she knows the sounds of letters but if he or she has been read to extensively. (pp. 78–79)

This view reiterates the opinion of Wells (1986). In his case study of Rosie, a child who apparently had not been read to once before starting school, he suggests that she needs a personal introduction to literacy through stories (p. 159). One-on-one read-alouds actively involve children in the reading. Many teachers, especially those with other adult helpers in the classroom, are able to provide one-to-one read-alouds on a regular basis in addition to the class read-alouds. During these one-to-one interactions, other children will place themselves close enough to be able to listen in to the stories; such is the power and enjoyment of the read-aloud.

How does literacy support happen through read-alouds? First, children learn about literacy because they have an adult providing a model of reading. The read-aloud provides at the simplest level an understanding of how print functions and how it is used (Strickland & Morrow, 1989). As children watch adults use books to read aloud, they quickly become aware of and knowledgeable about left-to-right and front-to-back directionality. Holdaway (1979) suggests that teachers use Big Books for read-alouds so all the children can see the print and follow that process of learning.

But children learn far more from read-alouds than how to use a book (Butler, 1998). Children learn about the structure of stories—the beginning, middle, and end. Furthermore, as Dombey (1988) indicates, children also learn new words, new sentences, and new discourse patterns. When the children have the opportunity to explore in writing the stories that have been read aloud with them, that learning is extended. Fox (1993) indicates how literature influences children's own storytelling. Her record of young children's storytelling demonstrates how the stories that children have heard feed into their own stories.

Children also develop a knowledge and understanding of letters and letter-sound relationships. So although Moustafa (1997) argues that the starting point for young children is hearing stories rather than learning letters, the children do learn about letters from stories. For example, it is not hard to imagine the learning about letters and sounds that might follow a reading and rereading of *Sniff-Snuff-Snap!* (Dodd, 1995), in which the consonant blend *sn* is so prominent. This learning would occur even though the emphasis would be on the enjoyment of this delightful story.

In Teale's (1984) analysis of the benefits that accrue from read-alouds, he includes the development of positive attitudes toward reading. In part, these attitudes originate from the shared enjoyment of the story. However, they also come from the way in which stories can provide tales about lives and events outside the child's own experience (Trelease, 1995). Read-alouds can encourage children's positive attitudes toward books because they offer the chance to learn about a wider world.

Organization of This Book

In order to look more closely at read-alouds, Chapter 1 explores the activity in a kindergarten classroom. It is not always possible to watch—or listen to—a read-aloud in a classroom, but this chapter enables us to enter the classroom and observe what takes place. It includes transcript excerpts from the teacher's story reading and the children's comments and questions. Subsequently, we also see how a number of activities develop from this lively, enjoyable read-aloud. The chapter ends with an examination of three steps teachers can follow to create their own successful read-aloud program in the classroom.

Chapter 2 considers the importance of narrative as a way of thinking. It suggests that read-alouds encourage children to think in a particular way as a means of constructing a sense of reality. Story also adds to children's literacy skills, supports their cultural heritage, and aids personal development. To achieve these benefits, children must hear high-quality books during read-alouds. This chapter explores the use of predictable storybooks with repetition, rhyme, and rhythm, and highlights the importance of poetry and nonfiction texts.

Chapter 3 notes how the read-aloud can support detailed learning about letter and word print features such as the alphabet, phonics, and spelling. The children's involvement with stories and the writing that follows creates numerous opportunities for them to think about graphophonic connections. The stories also provide a starting point for the teacher to create a word wall that aids the children's learning.

The children's interest in the read-aloud frequently leads them into other activities that link to the story. Chapter 4 discusses how role-playing, drawing and writing, making books, creating arts and crafts, making and using puppets, and singing songs and rhymes are all part of the children's response. Sometimes it is the teacher who encourages the children in that direction; on other occasions it is the children who immediately want to follow the reading in a particular way.

When the teacher reads aloud from a Big Book, the nature of the activity is transformed. All the children can see the print, so the teacher can emphasize print features. Shared readings with Big Books are featured in Chapter 5, along with sustained silent reading, individual reading, buddy reading, paired reading, guided reading, and literature circles.

In a similar manner, the stories, poems, and rhymes that have been read aloud provide a good starting point for shared writing to occur. Chapter 6 considers how the teacher demonstrates writing and the discussions that take place during that activity. Other linked activities such as interactive writing, guided writing, and individual writing are explored in this chapter.

The stories that are read aloud create opportunities for many different activities to take place. They also lead into other curriculum areas such as mathematics, science, and social studies. Often the children inquire about the facts that are contained within the stories. At other times the teacher plans to use the story as a starting point for a study in another curriculum area. Chapter 7 examines how stories can provide the stimulus for a range of questions to be explored.

The Afterword reminds us that a great deal of learning flows from stories that are read aloud. Teachers should ensure that a variety of possibilities exist for children to follow a well-read story and to find enjoyment in the process.

The opportunities for developing a curriculum from a read-aloud are almost limitless. At the same time, the teacher should be aware that the main objective is to provide interesting books for the children to engage their thinking and emotions. The activities that are developed from the story must not dampen the children's enthusiasm for stories and reading. Similarly, no story should be overused to the point at which the children become less enthusiastic about it, as Powell and Hornsby (1998) indicate:

> Since all text is language, all texts have numerous possibilities for highlighting different aspects of language. There is no need to milk a book dry of skills and bore your students in the process; it is better to use the skills possibilities available in a variety of literature and other authentic texts. (p. 84)

The secret of success with read-alouds rests with the sensitive adult at home and, subsequently, the professional approach of the teacher. With the right balance, read-alouds can help children improve their learning skills and develop a love of reading that will last a lifetime. The following chapters illustrate just how this works.

CHAPTER 1

Interactive Read-Alouds

Read-Alouds in a Kindergarten Classroom: One Example

It was almost the end of another busy day in a classroom of 30 kindergarten children in London. The teacher gathered the children around her and prepared to read a story.

Teacher: What do you think this book is about?

Ben: A caterpillar.

David: It's got lots of hairs.

Matthew: And green eyes.

Sophie: Why is it wearing shoes?

Teacher: They do look like shoes, but they are the caterpillar's feet. It's a story about a very hungry caterpillar, and the author is Eric Carle.

Ben: Yeah, those letters tell us.

The Very Hungry Caterpillar (Carle, 1969) has been—and continues to be—enjoyed by millions of children worldwide. The appealing nature of the main character, the rhythm and repetition of the text, and the trail of holes left by the caterpillar through the pages all add to the attraction.

Before the teacher began reading to the 5-year-old children in this classroom, she introduced the book to them. She encouraged them to make comments about the front cover and the caterpillar. She also told them the author's name. One of the children indicated where the teacher got that information. The read-aloud was already demonstrating what Strickland and Morrow (1989) describe as a "cooperative construction of meaning between the adult and child" (p. 323). The literacy event was interactive, and the children were encouraged to participate with comments and questions.

The children's involvement was maintained as the teacher started to read the first page:

Amy: I can see the moon.

Denise: It's smiling.

Teacher: It does look like it's smiling.
In the light of the moon
a little egg lay on a leaf.

Sally: I can see it; it's white.

Teacher: It is, isn't it?

Subsequently, when the teacher reached the pages where the caterpillar eats a different fruit on each day from Monday to Friday, there was great excitement:

Danny: There are lots of holes in the book.

John: And fruit.

Teacher: Yes, there are different fruits with holes. I wonder why there are holes in the fruit?

Ben: That's where the caterpillar eats.

John: He nibbles holes.

Matthew: I like fruit.

Stephanie: So do I.

Teresa: I like strawberries.

Teacher: Yes, I thought you would, and so did the very hungry caterpillar.
On Monday
he ate through
one apple.
But he was still
hungry.

The holes in the book almost inevitably intrigue children. The five different fruits also tend to bring forth comments, as shown here when the teacher encouraged the children to take part in the read-aloud by accepting their observations and responding to them. Furthermore, the teacher was able to use the comments to lead back into the reading of the story in a natural manner. Her actions contributed to the children's literacy learning and were an important part of the management of the class.

As the teacher continued with the story, the children extracted fine detail from the illustrations. For example, when they reached Thursday, one of the children commented on the strawberries:

Jamie: Four strawberries—one's upside down.

Teacher: There are four strawberries.
On Thursday
he ate through
four strawberries

When a child makes this sort of comment, it encourages others in the class to look carefully at the pictures and eventually at the print.

The children also made links from the story to their own feelings. As the teacher repeated the refrain, Ben expressed his own hunger.

Teacher: *but he was still*
hungry.

Ben: I'm hungry. Is it home time?

Teacher: Nearly; you'll soon be able to have a snack.

The Saturday two-page spread in the book would remind Ben even more that he was hungry. Other children also commented on the illustration that showed the food the caterpillar consumed on Saturday:

John: Look at all that food.

Danny: There's a lollipop. I like lollipops.

Following these comments, the teacher read the corresponding text and asked why the caterpillar ended up with a stomachache.

Ben: He had too much food.

Jamie: I like all that food

Amy: He was greedy.

Teacher: That's right; he ate too much. But what else gave it a stomachache?

Sophie:	Real caterpillars eat leaves.
Teacher:	Yes, they do, Sophie. The caterpillar ate the wrong food and it gave him a stomachache.
Joanne:	He needs medicine.
Ben:	My mum gives me stuff when I'm not well.
Teacher:	Yes, you have some medicine. Well...

> *The next day was Sunday again.*
> *The caterpillar ate through*
> *one nice green leaf*

Sophie:	Now he'll be better.
Teacher:	Yes.

> *and after that he felt*
> *much better.*

As this portion of the transcript demonstrates, the children remained very involved with the story and were able to relate it to events in their own lives. Indeed, the amount of interaction between the teacher and the children was greater than the time spent on the actual reading of the story. This is often the case, especially in the first read-aloud of a book, and particularly in a kindergarten or preschool classroom.

As the story reaches its conclusion, the caterpillar builds a cocoon. This development intrigued the children.

Samuel:	It looks like a stone.
Pavi:	That's a funny house.
Teacher:	Yes, it's a cocoon. And after he pushed his way out of the cocoon...

> *he was a beautiful butterfly!*

Danny:	That's pretty.
Teresa:	I saw a butterfly in my garden.
Teacher:	So you saw a beautiful butterfly in your garden?
Teresa:	Yes, but it wasn't all those colors. It was nearly all white.
Teacher:	Was it? I wonder what it looked like when it was a caterpillar.

Other children wanted to tell about seeing white butterflies and green caterpillars. As they left the classroom, they were still talking about the story, caterpillars and butterflies, and food to be eaten.

The 5-year-olds enjoyed the story. They contributed to the reading by asking questions, making comments, and relating the story to their own experiences, and they remained excited about the story. This example demonstrates the benefits of read-alouds and shows why teachers of young children use this literacy activity so frequently.

Many teachers read stories at the beginning of the day so they can capitalize on the children's excitement by providing immediate opportunities for them to explore the story in a variety of ways. In this example, the teacher chose to read the story at the end of the school day because she knew the children would talk about it at home and therefore develop their ideas about the content before returning to school.

Repeat Readings

The next morning, the teacher reminded the children of the story. The previous read-aloud and the children's subsequent talk and thinking about the story provided a strong background for the events of the day:

Teacher: Do you remember *The Very Hungry Caterpillar?*

Jamie: I liked that story.

Ben: He eat [sic] all the wrong food.

Teacher: He did. He ate all the wrong food.

Michael: He's got a funny face.

Danny: Read it again.

In this brief interaction, some of the children indicated their positive feelings toward the story and their recognition of a theme, and they requested another reading. The teacher was expecting this response and had made preparations for another reading and for other activities linked to the story.

During the repeat reading, the interactions continued to strengthen. The rhythm and repetition that are part of this story encouraged the children to take part in the reading. The teacher began the refrain and paused, which prompted the children to join in:

Teacher:	*On Monday* *he ate through* *one apple.* *But* [with emphasis and pausing for the children]
Children:	*he was still* *hungry.*
Matthew:	He eats lots of food.
Teacher:	He does. Now, *On Tuesday*

By the time the teacher reached the Friday page, all the children were anticipating the refrain and joining in, and they were doing so earlier by starting with *but*.

The children were also excited to give their opinions about the caterpillar and the foods he ate on Saturday.

Danny:	He got a bellyache.
Anna:	He eats the wrong food.
Ben:	He eat [sic] people's food.
Amy:	He was greedy. [A repeat of her comment from the previous day, now given with some emphasis.]
Matthew:	He should have just eaten leaves.

Heath (1982, 1983) argues that as children participate in interactive story readings, they learn not only how to take meaning from books but how to talk about it. During these interactions, the children are able to provide "what-explanations," such as a description of what the topic is about. Subsequently, this provides the basis for the children to provide explanations and affective commentaries. Although Heath suggests that these are requirements for the upper grades of school, this also can occur with younger children. In this example, Amy provided a reason why the caterpillar got a stomachache, and Matthew suggested how the caterpillar could have avoided the problem. The interactive nature of the read-aloud supports and encourages this type of thinking.

The children also remained very interested in the cocoon. They wanted to talk about the cocoon and to relate that to their own home and other types of houses.

Joanne:	He made a special house for himself.
Matthew:	Yeah, a cocoon.
Sally:	I live in a house.
Lewis:	I live in a flat.
Sophie:	My rabbit lives in a hutch.
Teacher:	Well done. People and animals live in different types of homes, and the caterpillar made his own house—a cocoon.

In this exchange, the teacher indicated that she welcomed comments during the read-aloud. In doing so, she encouraged a pattern of interactive read-alouds in the future. She confirmed the children's comments about the different types of houses that people and animals inhabit, and she reminded them that the caterpillar built his own house. She also repeated the name of that house: a cocoon.

This read-aloud gave the children the opportunity to behave like readers. Furthermore, their memorization of parts of the story helped them in the days and months ahead when they looked through the book on their own and started to read the print. In these ways, the read-aloud provided a foundation for literacy learning.

After completing the story, the teacher asked the children what they liked about it. She prompted the class to reflect on the story and their feelings toward it. There were many responses:

Danny:	I liked it when he made holes in the fruit. He crawled in and out.
Ben:	I liked the bit where he eat [sic] all the wrong food and gave him a tummyache.
Joanne:	It tells us all about the butterfly.

These responses—along with the children's comments during the repeat reading, their contributions to the reading, and their excitement about the story at the start of the day—all suggested that they had benefited from the two readings and that they would be interested in following the story with other activities.

Activities After the Read-Aloud

During the next few days, the children explored the story in a number of ways. Some of the activities were suggested by the teacher and others came from the children themselves.

Stick puppets. The children made caterpillars out of dough, clay, cloth, or cardboard. The teacher also helped the children construct caterpillar stick puppets, which generated future interest in creating stick puppets of other creatures or characters. She encouraged the children to use the puppets throughout the day as she reread parts of the story.

Other children painted large pictures of chocolate cake, ice cream cones, and the rest of the inappropriate food the caterpillar ate on Saturday. The teacher added large printed labels for each of those foods. Each time the teacher recited that part of the story and the children joined in, the children moved the puppets along the posters to crawl from one food to another.

What did this mean for the children's incidental learning? They memorized another part of the story, recalled the sequence of foods eaten on the Saturday, matched the book illustrations and student paintings to the story as it was recited, noted the teacher's large printed words under each picture, and worked collaboratively. They also had great fun.

Additional readings. In addition to encouraging the children to use their puppets beside the posters, the teacher read the complete story many times because the children enjoyed hearing it so much and often requested it. Those additional readings enabled the children to gain ownership of the story. They grew confident in their knowledge of the story, became familiar with the main character, and could recall some of the key phrases for themselves. A few children were able to recite much of the story on their own.

The frequent repeat readings of the book took place quite naturally within the classroom. As Teale and Sulzby (1989) argue, "Repeated readings by the teacher are especially important" (p. 7). They replicate the valuable repeat readings that many children enjoy at home (Campbell, 1999), and they encourage the children to read the book for themselves. Children enjoy having the stories repeated because it enables them to gain ownership of the words and meanings of the book. As Morrow (1988) notes, repeat readings lead the children to fo-cus on print as well as story structure. As the children begin to memo-rize many of the book's words, they are able to look at each page and recall some of the story. They can take part in the reading by offering some words, phrases, and sentences as the adult reads aloud. In this way, they are able to behave like readers.

Singing rhymes. Throughout the day as we listen to young chil-dren engaged in various activities, we can hear echoes of the story from the read-aloud. In this classroom the children often repeated key phrases, such as "but he was still hungry," as they drew and painted. Their involvement with the story also extended into other linked rhymes, verses, or songs.

To continue the shared book experience, the teacher used a song poster with large print as the basis for another literacy activity. As Holdaway (1979) notes, "Some of [the] instructional reading material can be their songs—and poems" (p. 66). The teacher had prepared a poster with the words to a simple song that linked closely to *The Very Hungry Caterpillar.* In the song, the caterpillar is eating, and there is a sequence of eggs, caterpillar, pupa or cocoon, and butterfly, then back to eggs. The teacher followed the sequence with the children as she sang with them and pointed to the words on the poster:

I went to the cabbages one day.
What do you think I saw?
Eggs in a cluster, yellow as a duster.
What could it all be for?

I went to the cabbages one day.
What do you think I saw?
Caterpillar crawling, caterpillar munching.
What could it all be for?

I went to the cabbages one day.
What do you think I saw?
I saw a super duper pupa.
What could it all be for?

I went to the cabbages one day.
What do you think I saw?

I saw a butterfly flutter by.
What could it all be for?

I went to the cabbages one day.
What do you think I saw?
Eggs in a cluster, yellow as a duster.
What could it all be for?

As we expect from such events, the children soon picked up the words of the song. The first, second, and fourth lines are repeated in each verse, and the third line shows the life cycle of the butterfly, which the children had followed previously in Carle's story. Within a few repeats of the song, the children were joining in well and with great enthusiasm. Songs such as this become a valuable resource for the teacher, and a collection of verses and songs that complement read-alouds can be developed over time.

The teacher also printed a short verse as a large poster. In this kindergarten classroom she used it with the children as a poem to be recited:

"Who's that tickling my back?"
said the wall.
"Me," said a caterpillar,
"I'm learning to crawl."

Subsequently, it was not difficult for the teacher to involve small groups of children to act out the words. With some children as the wall, others as the caterpillar, and groups to recite the verse, the children engaged again with the antics of a caterpillar. They also made connections between the words they recited and the print on the poster. By this time the printed word *caterpillar* had been seen, spoken, and enjoyed in many different contexts. Many children were starting to recognize the word.

Drawing and writing. In addition to making the two posters, the teacher also created a small word wall. This ensured that some of the words from the story were readily available for the children in the classroom. The word wall was especially useful for some of the children as they began to draw and write. Others needed to make less reference to the word wall because they were confident about taking risks with words, which the teacher encouraged. These children produced their writing with their own invented spellings based on the sounds they heard in each word as they wrote.

Because of the nature of the story, many of the children produced drawings or collages of the caterpillar (see Figure 1). Additionally, some children included what the caterpillar ate. Others extended that line of thinking and drew pictures of different animals and what they liked to eat. Two of the children's drawings demonstrate this (see Figures 2 and 3).

Their writing also indicates their varying levels of understanding about print. In the example in Figure 2, the child produced four words: *A graff ates leves* (A giraffe eats leaves). One of the words is written conventionally, and the other three are close enough approximations to

---

FIGURE 1
Sample Caterpillar Collage

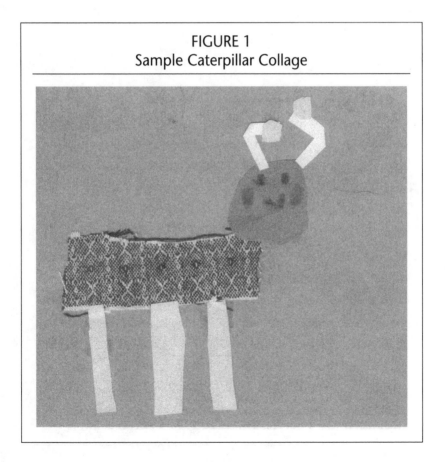

enable the reader to make sense of the child's effort. In particular, *graff* and *leves* demonstrate a good use of the graphophonic features and the child's growing knowledge of letters and sounds. Furthermore, each of the words appears within a space. The spacing can be contrasted with the example in Figure 3, where the writing of *CABET FS* (Crab eats fish) is more difficult to decipher, although the picture clue helps the reader. In

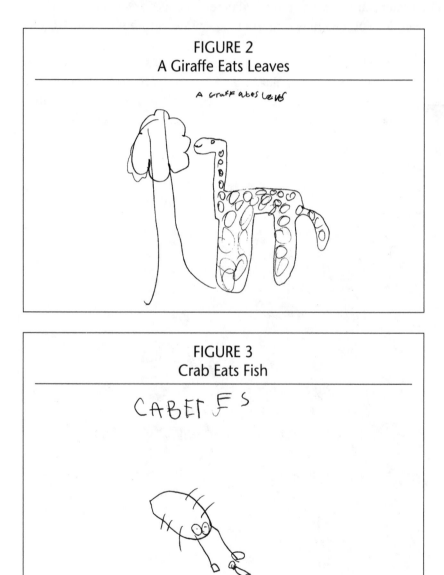

FIGURE 2
A Giraffe Eats Leaves

FIGURE 3
Crab Eats Fish

Figure 3, the final word is separated from the other two words, which shows that the child, not quite 5 years old, had some knowledge of letters and sounds and was able to put that knowledge to good use while writing.

Other children stayed more firmly with the story they had heard. They wrote the story in their own words, although often in a very shortened form. For instance, as we see in Figure 4, Carly wrote only one sentence. It is evident that she used the word wall; each word is written conventionally.

FIGURE 4
Carly's Story

Other children retold the story in their own words or wrote about some part of the story. A few children let their imagination extend their view of the story. Richard linked the story to his other interests when he wrote about railways and roads (see Figure 5).

The teacher extended the link from the read-aloud to the children's writing by developing a class book. That book, titled *Our Caterpillar Stories* (see Figure 6), was placed in the classroom library alongside *The Very Hungry Caterpillar*.

FIGURE 5
Richard's Story

In each of these ways, the children remained involved with the story they had enjoyed.

Focus on the life cycle (science). *The Very Hungry Caterpillar* is an ingenious book in several ways. In addition to providing a captivating story (Trelease, 1995), it teaches children about the days of the week and the sequence of those days, and it encourages them to think about the numbers 1 through 5. In addition, it follows the life cycle of the butterfly. Once the story has been read a number of times, the children are knowledgeable about that aspect of science.

The song also added to the children's scientific awareness. As the song was sung in the classroom for the second time, one of the children commented, "This song can go on forever." A few of the children, supported by the teacher, folded a sheet of paper into four sections and drew pictures of the cycle with eggs, caterpillar, cocoon, and butterfly. That led the children to re-create the science sequence and follow a simple story structure of beginning, middle, and end.

Counting and measuring (mathematics). Although the text encouraged the children to count from 1 to 5 with each of the weekday pages, the teacher used the children's interest in the main character to measure, compare, and count beyond 5. For instance, the children took great delight in drawing pictures of the caterpillars. They liked to follow the example set by Eric Carle and include bold facial features. Adrian's picture of the caterpillar (see Figure 7) seemed to capture the main character particularly well.

As the children drew caterpillars, the class discussed their various lengths. Questions such as "How long is your caterpillar?" and "Who has got the longest caterpillar?" led the children to count with cubes and compare them with others. Adam used his picture to measure the length of the caterpillar. He wrote that "my caterpillar si [is] 14 squares long." To make that calculation, he placed 14 math cubes beside his picture and counted them. His colored picture accurately reflects the

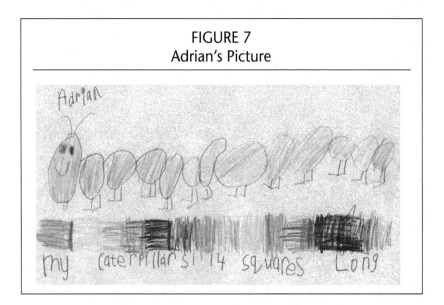

FIGURE 7
Adrian's Picture

number and colors of the 14 squares he used. Throughout this process, the children remained excited about their drawings and engaged incidentally in mathematical thinking.

Read-Alouds in the Classroom: Getting Started

It takes work to ensure that the read-aloud is successful. As the kindergarten example shows, the teacher has to prepare for the read-aloud, read the book as a performance, and ensure that the children take part. The remainder of this chapter can help teachers get started.

Preparing for a Read-Aloud

Because there are so many books available, teachers may be tempted to pick one up at the last minute to read aloud to the class. However, the experience of reading aloud quickly demonstrates the need for a more adequate preparation. Wade (1990) suggests that "stories need to be introduced, presented, recommended, talked over and savored together" (p. 31). This implies that teachers need to prepare for a read-aloud just like other aspects of the curriculum.

Graham and Kelly (1997) provide a read-aloud checklist separated into four main headings: select, plan, practice, and deliver. For their plan, Graham and Kelly suggest six areas that might need to be considered:

1. deciding on any resources that might be needed,
2. how much is to be read,
3. how will the book be introduced,
4. points the teacher might raise for discussion,
5. how to conclude the session, and
6. what might be used in reserve if time is available at the end of the read-aloud. (p. 63)

None of these issues need to consume much of the teacher's time. But the list does indicate that the teacher will need to be prepared for the read-aloud.

Trelease (1995) also comments on the preparation for the read-aloud. Perhaps his most important point is that teachers need to preview the book by reading it to themselves before the session. This ensures that the book is known and is appropriate for the children. Trelease suggests choosing a book that matches the intellectual, social, and emotional level of the audience. This is not easy, but teachers will be aware of the books the children enjoy, and they will become increasingly competent at making the link between text and audience. The preview of the book also ensures that the adult can read it with an awareness of the flow of the text. Even the most experienced teachers find that for the read-aloud to be successful, a practice read is helpful. This is so even when the teacher has already read the book to another class. The practice serves as a reminder of the actual words, the page turning, particular key phrases, and the need for emphasis. When that practice has taken place, the read-aloud is likely to be a worthwhile performance that captures the children's interest.

Reading the Book as a Performance

In the reality of the classroom, it can be difficult to get the children settled for a story. Mood is important, and the teacher needs to attempt to settle the children without the use of authoritarian requests to pay attention. Equally, the read-aloud should not be used as part of a threat, such as indicating that there will be no story if there is too much noise. The read-aloud is too important to be missed. Once the read-aloud is established as an enjoyable and exciting part of the day, the children are likely to settle quickly for the story. This enjoyment is even more likely if the children can sense the teacher's enthusiasm for books. Many teachers get the children's attention by indicating that they have another exciting book to read. Neuman (1998) suggests starting with a song, a finger play, or a brief chant to signal the time for a read-aloud. Some teachers use music to set the mood and tone.

Trelease (1995) has noted further useful points teachers should consider to ensure the quality of read-alouds. He suggests that teachers

ensure that all the children can see any pictures easily,

sit with their head just above the children's heads so their voice will carry to all the children,

use plenty of expression when reading, and

adjust the pace of the reading to fit the story.

The main suggestion that Trelease makes is to avoid reading too quickly, which he suggests is the most common mistake in reading aloud. Reading at the right pace, pausing for effect, and creating an emphasis are all parts of the read-aloud that are likely to captivate the audience and extend their interest in story and literacy.

Ensuring That the Children Take Part

The interactive aspect of the read-aloud provides many benefits for young children. In the kindergarten classroom shown earlier, the children made comments about the story and the illustrations:

John: He nibbles holes.

Amy: I can see the moon.

They also related the text to their own experiences:

Matthew: I like strawberries.

And they demonstrated their knowledge:

Sophie: Real caterpillars eat leaves.

Engaging in this type of talk enables the children to understand the story, to extract meanings, and to clarify their own thinking. As Dombey (1988) notes, the children become "partners in the telling" (p. 75). This is so even though the children may not yet be able to read the print and have not seen the book before.

The children's comments and questions during the reading should not unnerve teachers. The students' curiosity and interest is fostered when the teacher answers their questions and responds to their comments. Dombey (1988) extends this view by suggesting that the teacher needs to invite the children to join in the reading as active participants. The kindergarten teacher did this very effectively:

Teacher: I wonder why there are holes in the fruit?

Then later:

Teacher: What else gave it a stomachache?

Such questions encouraged the children to participate, and it was evident that they had become used to contributing as they made numerous comments.

Additionally, the teacher also can encourage children to participate in the actual reading of the text. This is especially the case, of course, with those parts of the text where there is a repetition of words:

Teacher: *On Monday*
he ate through
one apple.
But [with emphasis and pausing for the children]
Children: *he was still*
hungry.

Inviting the children into the read-aloud to say some of the text is useful. It encourages them to behave like readers, and it provides a foundation for their individual involvement with a book.

After the comments, questions, and participation, the teacher recreates a focus on the book again and resumes reading. This is not easy. It is developed by changing the emphasis in the voice, pausing, and using signals for the children, such as "On the next page" or "Now." Most teachers of young children are able to perfect this skill so that the read-aloud flows from reading to active participation and back to reading.

Of course, the teacher contribution is not always verbal. Facial expressions can encourage participation or suggest a continuation of the story. Similarly a finger on the lips may indicate a return to the story. These nonverbal behaviors are designed to encourage the children's participation in the read-aloud, to signal a reading from the book, and in some circumstances, to remind one or more children of appropriate behavior.

After the reading, the children also can participate by taking part in a class discussion. As Trelease (1995) notes, this gives time for the children's thoughts, hopes, fears, and discoveries to surface. At the same time, he reminds us that such discussions should not be turned into a quiz or an attempt to pry story interpretations from the child. Rather, talking about the book helps the children create meanings (McGee, 1995). The discussion also can be the springboard that takes the children from the story into other activities.

This glimpse inside a kindergarten classroom provides a good indication of how teachers might work with young children during a read-aloud. Of course, aspects of the read-aloud vary as teachers work with preschoolers or with Grade 3 students. In preschool, the dialogue between the teacher and children is often longer and less focused, and the teacher may need to work harder to respond to the children's comments and use them to return to the reading. In contrast, the older children are often more willing to listen to the entire story, saving their comments until the end of the read-aloud. Then their interest in following aspects of the story in pictures and writing is frequently extensive.

Routman (1991) refers to the read-aloud in the classroom as "the single most influential factor in young children's success in learning to read" (p. 32). The interactive nature of read-alouds provides a major support for the children's literacy learning. Through the use of questions and statements from both adult and child, each passage is clarified and integrated with other parts of the story. Young children can anticipate, or predict, upcoming story events with the knowledge they acquire. This experience helps them develop strategies for making inferences and hypotheses both for the book being read and for other written language. In this kindergarten classroom, the children enjoyed the read-aloud, became involved in the story, participated in a related discussion, and used the meanings and the words to extend their excitement into other aspects of learning.

As Routman (1991) notes, some teachers feel uncomfortable about devoting a great deal of time to read-alouds. The children and teacher enjoy the activity so much, it may not seem like sufficiently hard work. However, the children's enjoyment forms the basis for learning about stories and reading, learning to read, learning through literacy, and wanting to read (Short, 1999). Because of these numerous benefits, read-alouds should take place every day.

CHAPTER 2

The Importance of Narrative and Quality Books

Narrative and story are central features in the early years of education (Whitehead, 1987). A particular benefit of story is that it provides a way of organizing thinking about experiences and making those meaningful. Bruner (1968) argues that there are two modes of thoughts—"a good story and a well-formed argument" (p. 99)—that provide different ways of viewing reality. Both are important, although this book focuses on narrative.

As children transact with stories (Rosenblatt, 1978), they consider the development of the action, and they begin to develop an awareness of what the protagonists and antagonists involved in the action know, think, or feel. These transactions enable children to build what Langer (1995) refers to as an envisionment; that is, the understanding they have about the text. This envisionment, or understanding, will be subject to change as ideas unfold and new ideas come to mind. During a read-aloud, story is a basis for encouraging thinking as the children interact with the adult. For example, in Chapter 1, as the children heard multiple readings of *The Very Hungry Caterpillar* and engaged in activities related to the story, they extended their thinking and developed their ideas.

At the same time, Whitehead (1997) reminds us that pleasure is "the first and all-pervasive theme in the world of literature" (p. 119). This pleasure is evident in classrooms where teachers and children share stories, particularly in classrooms where an initial emphasis on the story is key. Following the story with related activities, as shown in Chapter 1, also adds to the children's enjoyment.

When there is pleasure from the story, play and learning will come naturally and inevitably as the children construct meaning to what they have heard and considered. Dorothy White (1954/1984) provides numerous examples of how her preschool daughter Carol used a story line as the basis for her play at home. For instance, when Carol was almost 4 years old, Dorothy read her a book titled *The Little Train* (Lenski, 1946). In that story, the key character is Engineer Small, who has to ensure that the train is ready for its journey. Subsequently, Carol "played trains" on a regular basis. White notes, "Carol oils wheels, shovels coal, reads her orders, pulls a whistle-cord and makes off from the sofa station for the tunnel under the table" (p. 83). From that play, Carol was able to extend her understanding of railways and construct her own meanings onto the story. As Phillips and McNaughton (1990) suggest, children who have had frequent storybook readings at home also learn how to construct meaning from unfamiliar texts.

In Whitehead's (1987) discussion, she suggests that there are three main strands—skills, cultural heritage, and personal development—to support the claims that narrative and story bring benefits to young children. These strands are interrelated, and often all three are apparent at any one time.

Skills

Children who have a substantial number of encounters with books at home learn how to manipulate and use a book in their first few years. For instance, in a longitudinal study of story readings with my granddaughter Alice, I note that by age 12 months,

> Alice could handle a book by:
> picking it up or extracting one from a bookshelf,
> orienting the book correctly so it was the right way up,
> turning a page when she wanted to look at the next picture,
> turn the pages from the front towards the back. (Campbell, 1999, p. 17)

This is typical of many children who are given similar opportunities to explore books; they see demonstrations of reading by adults and are supported by adults as they manipulate books. In the classroom, the adult demonstrations that occur as part of a read-aloud ensure that even children with very limited book experience learn these skills.

Children also learn about the language of print from stories, and they gain an understanding of the structure of stories—beginning, middle, and end—as well as an understanding about characters, setting, and plot. Carol Fox (1993) provides evidence of that learning in her study of the oral storytelling of five preschool children. Transcripts of these retellings demonstrate their learning. For instance, Fox notes that when Justine was 4 years, 1 month old, she related the following story:

> Once upon a time there were two little dicky birds in a tree
> and mammy one said "Don't go out there"
> but the naughtiest was the little baby one
> he went out 'cos he didn't listen to his mum
> she said "There's wolves out there and foxes and
> ugly lions and other sorts of things that will
> eat the birds and crawling insects and
> spiders and witches"
> and he flyed out of the nest
> and one of the tigers opened his mouth and
> gobbled him all up
> and the second little baby came to eat him up
> and that's the end of the story. (p. 85)

In her detailed analysis of this story, Fox notes that the actions happen in the past tense and the mother bird speaks in the present tense. Although this is a simple story structure, it contains two actions and causal resolutions, and it was not Justine's richest narrative. Nevertheless, that storytelling and others like it demonstrate a wealth of learning about language.

Children can extend their understanding of language when they have the opportunity to write about aspects of the stories they've heard in read-alouds or to rewrite the stories in their own words. Additionally, children learn about letters and letter-sound relationships from stories. This subject is discussed in more detail in Chapter 3.

Cultural Heritage

Children learn about a wider world from narrative, especially through the oral tradition of nursery rhymes, singing games, and chants (Opie & Opie, 1959), as well as the folk tales and fairy tales that are handed from one generation to another. Then there is the "received" literature (Whitehead, 1987), which includes books that are read in succeeding generations and serve as a link to our past.

When children engage with the narrative of nursery rhymes, they enjoy the rhythm and rhyme. They also learn about story structure and acquire an understanding of onset and rime, which teachers can capitalize on later. Furthermore, within those nursery rhymes, there are often links with the past:

> Ring-ring o'roses
> A pocket full of posies.
> A-tishoo! A-tishoo!
> We all fall down.

This rhyme provides a startling reminder of the bubonic plague. Although most young children cannot make this connection, many teachers find it useful to return to the familiar nursery rhymes in a later grade and to begin to explore the rhymes' origins.

Children are likely to meet some of the fairy tales in a variety of formats. For instance, in Janet and Allan Ahlberg's (1978) *Each Peach Pear Plum*, there are merely short references to key characters:

> Cinderella on the stairs
> I spy the Three Bears

Nevertheless, the detailed pictures beside each rhyme encourage young children to think and talk about those characters, which can lead to more extended readings of the fairy tales from other books.

In recent years, a number of picture books have become part of a new collection of received literature. For example, *The Very Hungry Caterpillar* (Carle, 1969) has been read aloud with—and read by—millions of children worldwide. It is book that is read to children by parents who enjoyed it in their own childhood, and it appears to continue to captivate children today. Not only is it part of a received literature, but it also expands a child's world. The story of the life cycle is learned as well as the tale about the hungry caterpillar.

Tizard and Hughes (1984) examine the responses of 4-year-old Rosy, who was sharing a book with her mother and thus exploring aspects of a wider world. The title of the book is not indicated, but the plot involves a puffin that witnesses a shipwreck. Here is a portion of the transcript:

> Child: Do, um boats, when they're on, right on the sea break like that?
>
> Mother: Well, not very often, but sometimes they do. If the weather's very bad, and they get thrown against the rocks, they do break up. (p. 63)

Because the family was planning a summer holiday from England to France, Rosy found this response unsettling:

> Child: I, I, I, don't want to. I'm not going, but we won't go on, if there's too many people on the boat we won't go on it, will we? (p. 63)

Rosy talked about boats, discussed the possibility of shipwrecks, and made a connection to a possible sea trip. Such explorations clarify children's thinking and help them "develop a much richer mental model of the world" (Wells, 1986, p. 152), which further emphasizes the importance of read-alouds at home and in school.

Personal Development

A number of educators have written about the power of stories and the importance of narrative for young children. For example, Kirby (1995) writes,

> The power of stories lies in the opportunities they provide for extending children's thinking and feeling in numerous ways including:
>
> their beliefs, assumptions, attitudes, values about life, situations and people;
>
> their thinking and responses to everyday life and complex issues;
>
> their concerns, fears, pain, growing up, feelings and compassion for others;
>
> their relationships with other people;
>
> their knowledge of and responses to both their own culture and the culture of others;
>
> their imagination, enjoyment and satisfaction;
>
> their abilities to predict, question, hypothesize about situations and people;

the power to create and shape through their own stories;

the opportunity to talk to adults and peers about stories in an atmosphere which is collaborative, supportive and "risk free." (pp. 7–8)

Such a substantial listing creates two immediate impressions. First, it suggests a wider area of learning beyond helping children become readers. Second, it considers the many aspects of thinking and feeling that are supported by narrative.

I discovered a simple example of this intellectual and emotional engagement (Campbell, 1999) as my granddaughter Alice provided a memorized reading of *Sniff-Snuff-Snap!* (Dodd, 1995). The plot involves a warthog that attempts to restrict the use of a waterhole by other animals. After chasing away various animals, the warthog always returns to the waterhole. At the age of 4 years, 7 months, Alice relied on her memory of previous story readings and was able to recite the correct words about the warthog's last return as we looked at the final pages of the book:

Alice: *Back came the warthog,*
tired and hot,
for a long,
cool drink
at his favourite spot.
Down past rocks
and thornbush tree,
he came to the waterhole
BUT
what did he see?
THICK
BROWN
MUD. (Campbell, 1999, p. 107)

Alice then demonstrated her thinking about the story and her feelings about the warthog by adding a final few lines. The final picture includes a drop of rain splashing on the warthog's back. So Alice added,

Drip, drop, drip.
The rain came down
and filled up the waterhole again. (p. 108)

In creating that ending, Alice demonstrated empathy for the warthog. She was also thinking through the consequences of the rainfall in that environment. Interestingly, her first line recaptures the rhythm of the title of the story with the use of the *dr* consonant blend. The frequent adult-child read-alouds of this book had enabled the young reader to gain ownership of the words. This supported her development toward becoming an independent reader. In addition, the quality of the narrative did far more for Alice: it encouraged her thinking and feelings about the characters and the plot, to which she responded creatively.

Numerous comments have been made about how narrative supports personal development. Wade (1990) refers to the sustenance of story, noting that quality texts provide "food for the mind and for the feelings" (p. 30). Evans (1998) explores children's thoughtful responses to key emotional issues that are present in some stories. In one instance, she studied Grade 2 children as they wrote about the death of a pet dog in response to a reading of the story *I'll Always Love You* (Wilhelm, 1985). The children discussed the sad parts of the story and related it to their own experiences. However, they concluded that although the death of Elfie, the dog, was sad, the story as a whole was not, because the dog had had a good life.

The intellectual and emotional sustenance that children receive from a story makes them want to go on reading (Bettelheim & Zelan, 1981). Ensuring that children want to continue reading, to move to other books, and to reflect on what is read is an aim for all teachers.

Quality Books

There are so many high-quality books written for young children, it's impossible to mention them all here. The range of availability and quality is indicated here partly by the presence of authors from four different English-speaking countries: Eric Carle from the United States; Lynley Dodd from New Zealand; Mem Fox, whose writing is centered on Australia; and Pat Hutchins from the United Kingdom. Some of the books by these four authors are cited frequently in *Read-Alouds With Young Children*, and books by other outstanding authors also are mentioned. This still does no more than touch the surface of the many worthwhile books that can be read aloud with young children.

A much wider range of books for young children is listed in various sources. In Trelease's (1995) *The Read-Aloud Handbook,* there are more than 100 pages that list and annotate useful books that can be read aloud. Cullinan (1989) also produced an annotated list in a chapter on literature for young children. In addition, there are children's books listed in other texts on literacy, such as Routman's *Invitations* (1991). Her list includes books that invite readers into print and other predictable books that help children develop early reading strategies. Professional journals such as *The Reading Teacher* often include lists of appropriate recent books to share with young children; a regular column on children's books started in September 1999 (Giorgis & Johnson, 1999), and it includes lists of books for reading aloud. The columnists also group books for particular purposes, such as "for inviting interaction" (p. 80). The Internet also has a number of Web sites that provide information on children's literature (Karchmer, 2000). In addition to those lists, teachers should look out for awards that are given annually to books for young children.

Predictable Books

Rhodes (1981) suggests that there are certain predictable books that enable young children at school to read right away, because of the children's knowledge of language and of the world that they bring to the task. She argues that in predictable books the "language flows naturally, and the vocabulary and content reflect what children know" (p. 513), so children are able to predict what the author is going to say and how it will be said.

The key characteristic of predictability, Rhodes argues, is the use of repetitive patterns. For example, in *Slinki Malinki, Open the Door* (Dodd, 1993), a story about a cat and a parrot, after each of the characters' mischievous adventures indoors, the text repeats this phrase:

Slinki Malinki
jumped high off the floor,
he swung on a handle
and opened
a door.

Children hearing this book in a read-aloud are quickly able to predict the next page as the main characters move from room to room.

Other characteristics of predictable books include familiar concepts, a good match between text and illustrations, rhyme, rhythm of language, the familiarity of the story or story line to the child, and the use of familiar sequences (Rhodes, 1981). What does this mean when books such as *Slinki Malinki* are read in a classroom? Children already know that cats may make a mess at home, so this story involves familiar concepts and therefore assists their understanding. The close match between the text and illustrations also supports this predictability.

Children bring other knowledge to school. Many children often arrive with some knowledge of folk tales, fairy tales, and songs. Therefore, when they meet Cinderella again, the familiarity of the characters aids the predictability. Some multilayered texts (Watson, 1993) make use of that familiarity. As noted earlier, in *Each Peach Pear Plum* (Ahlberg & Ahlberg, 1978), the characters from one familiar text meet characters from other texts:

> Cinderella on the stairs
> I spy the Three Bears

This theme runs throughout the story.

We have already seen how Eric Carle made use of the familiar sequence of numbers from 1 to 5 and the days of the week. In *The Very Hungry Caterpillar,* those two sequences are linked as the caterpillar eats his way through the fruits on each day of the week. The children bring some understanding and predictability of those familiar sequences to the read-aloud, and the story further develops their understanding. The children's knowledge of language and the world helps them create meanings from books, and the repetition, rhyme, and rhythm of the text—what Wade (1990) refers to as "the three R's" of language and story (p. 7)—support the young children's learning.

Repetition

Repetition that contributes to the story line helps children become good readers. Typically, the repetition involves a phrase or a sentence rather than a single word, which was prominent in some of the basal readers used in the past. In *Slinki Malinki, Open the Door*, the repeated sentence contributes greatly to the excitement of the story and the buildup toward the conclusion. The phrase appears 6 times in the book, on 6 of the 15 pages of print. The familiar repetition also aids children when they begin to read such texts for themselves.

Because the repetition of a phrase or sentence is an integral part of the story, children pick up the phrase very quickly. For instance, when Alice was 2 years, 9 months old, it took just one reading at home of *Good-Night Owl* (Hutchins, 1972) before she contributed a key repetition:

Grandfather: *Owl*
Alice: *tried to sleep.*
Grandfather: *The bees buzzed,*
                buzz buzz,
                and
Alice: *owl tried to sleep.* (Campbell, 1999, p. 59)

Although Alice had not begun to give a great deal of attention to the print in books, she did use that key phrase when she attempted to construct the story by herself immediately after hearing the story for a second time:

Alice: *Owl tried to sleep*
                There's the bees,
                Owl tried to sleep
                and
                    the bees buzzed
                    buzz buzz.
                Owl tried to sleep
                and the squirrel was sitting in the tree.

While repetition contributes to the story line, it builds up the predictability and helps children toward ownership of the text. In addition, it supports young readers when they attempt to construct the story for themselves or move toward reading a well-known book on their own.

Rhyme

A number of picture books include a rhyme element, which most children love. For instance, in *Hairy Maclary from Donaldson's Dairy* (Dodd, 1983), the main characters are introduced one by one in an extending rhyme to eventually include the following:

Schnitzel von Krumm
with a very low tum,
Bitzer Maloney
all skinny and bony,
Muffin McLay
like a bundle of hay,
Bottomley Potts
covered in spots,
Hercules Morse
as big as a horse
and Hairy Maclary
from Donaldson's dairy.

Young children greatly enjoy that story, and within minutes they are usually keen to join in with the rhyme. Subsequently, it is not surprising that they can be heard using the rhymes as they engage with other activities in the classroom. And any sighting of a Dalmatian dog is almost certain to be referred to as a "Bottomley Potts covered in spots."

Children's enjoyment of rhymes in story is a continuation of the pleasure many of them experienced as they learned nursery rhymes at home or in a preschool. Not only do children like to hear rhymes, they also enjoy playing with words and using those words to create their own rhymes or jingles (Chukovsky, 1963). Teachers can capitalize on this interest in the classroom, first by providing worthwhile books for read-alouds and then by using that learning as a basis for phonological development. As Meek (1990) indicates, when children have fun with rhymes, phonology is developed. For example, with *Hairy Maclary from Donaldson's Dairy,* the play with rhyme leads to an awareness of onset (*kr* and *t*) and rime (*umm* and *um*), as in *Krumm* and *tum*. That awareness, Goswami and Bryant (1990) suggest, is a significant feature of children's development as readers.

A brief look at a few lines from one of Dr. Seuss's books, such as *Green Eggs and Ham* (1960), illustrates how children will be made aware of onset and rime:

That Sam-I-am!
That Sam-I-am!
I do not like
that Sam-I-am!

Do you like
green eggs and ham?

And later in the rhyme:

Would you eat them
in a box?
Would you eat them
with a fox?

In the first instance, the rime element *am* together with the onset letters *S* and *h* become very much part of the children's language and awareness. Then the rime *ox* together with the onset *b* and *f* are among the many others that are introduced. But mainly the children enjoy the nonsense of the repeating rhyme throughout the book.

Rhythm

Rhythm is an important feature of books for young children. The use of rhyme and repetition in *Green Eggs and Ham* creates a rhythm that children listen to and like to use themselves. It is doubtful if any of us have heard a reading of that book in which the reader does not create an almost song-like rhythm with the words. Children enjoy the rhythms that are created by the repetition and rhyme.

Rhythm in stories is an attraction for children, and this rhythm is produced in a variety of ways in the books that are read aloud. In *The Very Hungry Caterpillar*, a two-page spread highlights the foods the caterpillar ate on Saturday:

On Saturday
he ate through
one piece of
chocolate cake,
one ice-cream cone,
one pickle,
one slice of Swiss cheese,
one slice of salami....

There is a repetition of *one* on this first page of text that is repeated another five times on the opposite page as other foods are introduced.

However, it is the listing of the foods that appears to give the rhythm to the text. The alliteration, such as in *slice of salami*, adds a rhythmic feel to the text and attracts the children to the words.

The image created by the sounds in *slice of salami* can remain prominent in children's minds. In another kindergarten classroom I observed (Campbell, 1992), 5-year-old Richard read this book to his teacher in an individual reading conference. The correct reading of each miscue follows in parentheses:

Richard: *one slice of salami (Swiss) cheese*
            one slice of salami
            one lollipop

and then at the end of that double page

one slice of salami (watermelon). (p. 24)

Richard miscued *Swiss* and *watermelon* as the memory and rhythm of *slice of salami* dominated part of his reading.

Fox (1993) notes the importance of rhythm in some of the story-telling of preschoolers. One of the children in her study, Josh, heard radio weather reports on a regular basis. In the United Kingdom, these reports include conditions at sea at Fair Isle, Dogger Bank, and Rockall, as well as other areas. Josh caught the rhythm of those broadcasts and enjoyed producing his own weather reports.

Many teachers of young children seek predictability, repetition, rhyme, and rhythm in the books they read to the children. Others suggest different ways of looking for quality books. Nutbrown (1994) suggests that children's books should be looked at for their appeal, readability, content, development, and equal opportunities. Hart-Hewins and Wells (1990) suggest a somewhat similar list of content, language, attractiveness, and ease of reading. Teachers can add their own criteria to those lists based on their experience of reading to children and their discussion with colleagues about books. Each of these factors contributes to the wise selection of quality books for reading aloud with young children.

Poetry and Nonfiction

The emphasis in this chapter has been on the importance of narrative and children's engagement with stories through the use of high-

quality storybooks for read-alouds at home and in school. However, teachers of young children know that other texts are also important and have a place in read-alouds.

Some of the stories that are read to children might be regarded as extended poems. The rhyme and rhythm of many nursery rhymes, songs, and stories that are read aloud to children ensure that they enjoy hearing a variety of poetry read aloud as well. From these readings, children often like to move on to reading other poetry and to writing their own simple rhymes and poems.

In many stories there are also factual elements. For instance, in *Cimru the Seal* (Radcliffe, 1997), there is information beyond the story about the life of a seal, the seal's diet, and predators. The children learn much of that information incidentally, as the story is read aloud. However, in a Grade 2 classroom I observed, a discussion after the read-aloud demonstrated that the children were interested in exploring the factual aspects of the text. It is also important that teachers choose nonfiction books, or sections from them, as read-alouds from time to time. The children then have a model of that type of writing, and they can consider the "well-formed argument" (Bruner, 1968, p. 99).

Children are excited by the many different books that are read aloud to them. The read-alouds, and the activities that are linked to them, also facilitate the children's reading and writing. At the same time, the children also learn about print features, which is the subject of Chapter 3.

CHAPTER 3

Read-Alouds and Print Features

The excellent variety of storybooks that are available for read-alouds ensures that young children experience the widest possible contact with letters, sounds, and spellings. Studies of young children who have had frequent and regular read-alouds at home indicate that those children move on to school with a strong foundation of graphophonic knowledge (Campbell, 1999). The miscues these children produce as they read and the invented spellings they create as they write are indicators of this knowledge. For children in the early years of elementary school, classroom read-alouds provide a similar opportunity to learn about the alphabet, phonics, and spelling. As Kane (1999) argues, phonics can and should be taught from meaningful contexts: "The quality children's literature we want our children immersed in provides all the examples of phonics enthusiasts could ever want" (p. 771).

Just the titles of books such as *Hop on Pop* (Seuss, 1963) hint at the learning that is likely to take place as such books are shared with children. Part of this story rhyme reads,

We like to hop.
We like to hop
on top of Pop.
STOP
You must not
hop on Pop.

As children explore and think about writing, their awareness of sounds is enhanced. Singing, reciting, writing, and playing with words such as *hop*, *Pop*, *top*, and *stop* makes that so. As Strickland (1998) suggests, the children's involvement in rhymes, songs, and alliteration in

various links to read-alouds promotes phonemic awareness. It also provides the basis for learning the letters of the alphabet, phonics, and spelling.

Alphabet

Powell and Hornsby (1998) demonstrate that children using literature in a kindergarten class can consider graphophonic connections in a meaningful way. They show how one teacher used text from the storybook *Possum Magic* (Fox, 1983) to help the children think about a letter and then create an alliteration. The book reads,

> Later, on a beach in Perth, they ate a piece of pavlova.
> Hush's legs appeared. So did her body.
> "You look wonderful, you precious possum!" said Grandma Poss.

The teacher and the children used the alliteration to create a tongue twister: *The precious possum had a piece of pavlova in Perth.*

Subsequently, the teacher developed a chart of *p* words over a few days. She started with words from the story, and then the children suggested other words to add to the list. Together they created a form of word wall that used words from the read-aloud, children's forenames, and other words they found important: *Perth, pavlova, precious, possum, Patrick, party, puppy, Paul,* and *pink* (p. 86).

Staying with the theme, the teacher selected poems such as "Peter, Peter, Pumpkin Eater" to extend the children's attention to the letter. The <Pp> letter chart (with both uppercase and lowercase letters shown) was hung on the wall for the children to add other words beginning with *p*.

Then the class further developed the link with the story. As the possums continue their journey around Australia eating "people food," the story reveals,

> They ate Anzac biscuits in Adelaide,
> mornay and Minties in Melbourne,
> steak and salad in Sydney,
> and pumpkin scones in Brisbane.

Powell and Hornsby indicate how the first two lines formed the basis for two other letter charts. Again, the teacher began with words from the story and then included words from the children. These activities helped them learn the letters of the alphabet and move beyond that learning to consider the letters in greater detail.

Nonfiction alphabet books, such as *Animalia* (Base, 1986), can also add to the children's learning when they are used as the basis for a read-aloud. Furthermore, as Strickland (1998) notes, making those alphabet books readily available in the classroom for the children to browse through after a read-aloud furthers their interest and supports their learning.

Phonics

The fact that the children are learning phonics from read-alouds and the subsequent activities is made evident in numerous ways. For instance, during one kindergarten read-aloud of *When I Was Little Like You* (Walsh, 1997), one of the 5-year-olds in the class made an unexpected comment:

Teacher: *"When I was little like you," said Gran, "we bought fish from the boatman on the quay. A brace of bright mackerel for supper, still fresh and shining."*

Francis: You get a /k/ with three letters. Like in *quay*. You can have a *k*, *c*, or *q*.

The teacher had not taught these letters and letter sounds directly, but the constant play with language, words, and letters ensured that it was learned. The read-aloud led to a consideration of initial letter-sound correspondences as well as thinking about some words. It also gave the children a chance to initiate discussions about letter sounds.

In a first-grade classroom, the teacher read aloud the Big Book version of *Walking Through the Jungle* (Lacome, 1993), and encouraged the children to write a sentence with alliteration as a feature of their writing. Some of the children chose an animal from the story, such as the crocodile (see Figure 8).

In this writing, the child was able to produce alliteration, with each of the words spelled conventionally, although the child substituted *an* for *a*. Other children wrote about animals that were not part of the story, such as a flamingo (see Figure 9).

Although *fluffying* may not be a word, here it does appear to fit well with the description the child provided. As the word *flamingo* was not part of the story, it had to be written unseen by the child, who demonstrated a knowledge of letters and sounds and a willingness to construct words using that knowledge. When children are encouraged to write following read-alouds—and when their spellings are acknowledged for the learning that is demonstrated—then the foundations are in place for conventional spelling to develop, especially when the teacher and the children talk freely about letters, sounds, and words in context. As Geekie, Cambourne, and Fitzsimmons (1999) note, when children are encouraged to write from the very beginning of schooling, the need for the explicit teaching of phonics is reduced.

The alliteration writing activity, like many other literacy activities, encouraged the children to think about letters and sounds in the

---

FIGURE 8
Crocodile Sentence

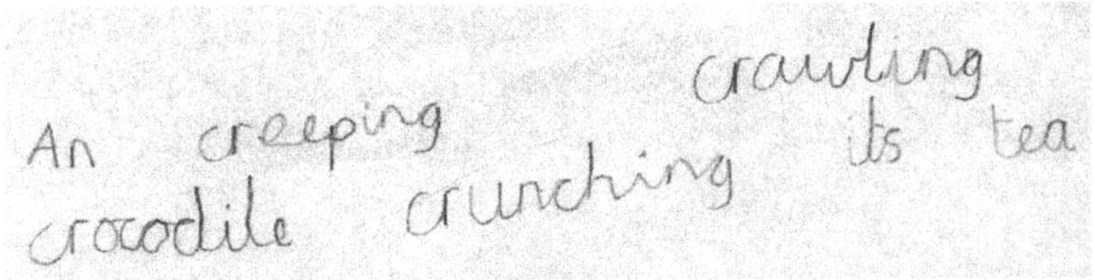

FIGURE 9
Flamingo Sentence

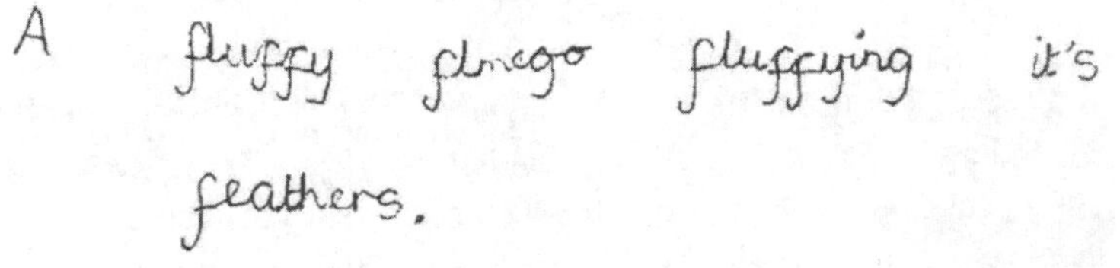

context of a story they enjoyed. There are numerous ways in which this can occur, and Opitz (2000) provides guidance about the possibilities. He includes a list of books that can serve as the basis for exploring alliteration and other aspects of letter-sound correspondences naturally as the stories are read aloud.

When children are encouraged to write in a variety of formats, they develop an understanding of phonics and a love of writing. Phinn (2000) suggests that young children should both listen to and write poems. "Miniature poems," such as the Japanese haiku, are manageable for children because of the length. Children in second grade and third grade respond well to the discipline of the haiku's short lines of five, seven, and five syllables. The writing also requires them to think carefully about letters and sounds as they consider the syllables in words. This builds on earlier work they may have done in the preschool and kindergarten classroom to clap out the syllables in their names and in nursery rhymes as part of a group or class activity (Ericson & Juliebö, 1998).

Word Wall

There has traditionally been a substantial amount of print on the walls of classrooms for young children. For instance, in Goddard's (1958) book on K–2 reading, the author presents many pictures that show simple print that was used to support children's reading and writing. Goddard argues that it is not sufficient just to have the print on the wall; the teacher has to talk with the children about that print.

In addition, the children in these classrooms had their own "wordbooks" (individual dictionaries). Throughout the year, the children expanded their dictionaries, adding words from the classroom print and reading books, and words they asked the teacher to help them spell correctly. The strategy supported children with a personal resource for words that might otherwise be a problem for them. However, it was difficult for the teacher to ensure that the dictionaries did not become overloaded with words that were seldom used. Furthermore, the teacher could not support every child as needed, and some important words were probably missed. The idea of a classroom dictionary or word wall attempts to meet these difficulties.

Cunningham and Allington (1999) provide an argument for word walls in kindergarten and other primary classrooms. Again, however, it is not enough for the teacher to hang a word wall in the classroom and suggest that the children use it as necessary. Instead, the authors argue, it is important for the teachers to "DO" word walls. In particular, they suggest that the teacher should adhere to a number of key points:

1. Being selective and "stingy" about what words go up there, limiting the words to those really common words that children need a lot in writing.

2. Adding them gradually—five a week.

3. Making them very accessible by putting them where everyone can see them, writing them in big black letters, and using a variety of colors so that the constantly confused words (*for*, *from*, *that*, *them*, *they*, *this*, etc.) are on different colors.

4. Practicing the words by chanting and writing them because struggling readers are not usually good visual learners and can't just look at and remember words.

5. Doing a variety of review activities to provide enough practice so that the words are read and spelled instantly and automatically.

6. Making sure that Word-Wall Words are spelled correctly in any writing the students do. (Cunningham & Allington, 1999, p. 136)

It is evident from the first and sixth points that the teacher does have to be very selective if the children are expected to spell those words correctly in any writing. However, these expectations may support the children in learning key high-frequency words so that their reading and writing is facilitated.

Many kindergarten teachers start word walls by placing each child's forename in the alphabetic word wall, which contains a section for each letter of the alphabet. Studies of individual children before they start school emphasize the importance of their ability to write their own name (e.g., Baghban, 1984; Campbell, 1999; Schickedanz, 1990), and inevitably, the children are interested in seeing their name on the wall. From this listing, the class can also make some comparisons. For example, it will be unusual for the classroom not to have two children's forenames starting with the same first letter. Then the teacher can expand the list by adding some of the key characters from storybooks or some of the high-frequency words, as suggested by Cunningham and Allington (1999). The use of a word wall supports the children's learning of the alphabet, recognition of each letter, and phonic knowledge of initial letter sounds.

Moustafa (1997) also advocates the use of word walls. However, she suggests creating those word walls more specifically from the predictable stories that are read aloud. In this case, the teacher asks the children to choose their favorite words from the story after a number of repeat readings. In order to support the children further, the teacher can place a logo from the story, perhaps of the key character, next to each word.

Additionally, the teacher can highlight certain letters of each word to emphasize the onset or rime—an important part of children's learning (Goswami, 1999). For a Humpty-Dumpty story with the words *wall* and *fall*, the teacher might highlight the onset /w/ or /f/, or the rime element /all/. The words can be regrouped frequently as the teacher talks with the children about words starting with /w/, or when the class is considering other /all/ rimes. As Moustafa (1997) indicates, such strategies make the phonics instruction "explicit, systematic and extensive" (p. 93).

For Moustafa, working in this way creates a whole-to-parts phonic instruction. However, it differs from traditional phonics instruction in that it follows, rather than precedes, the story. It is only after a story has been read to, with, and by children that parts of the words are taught. And it concentrates on units of the syllable—namely, letter-onset and letter-rime correspondences—rather than letter-phoneme correspondences.

Whichever approach is used, the word walls provide support in a number of ways:

- The children will learn about the letters of the alphabet as each section has a space available for words to be added.
- The sequence of the alphabet is shown by the word wall, and the teacher can bring the children's attention to that feature (as well as singing some of the well-known alphabet songs).
- The high-frequency key words can become part of child's visual memory of words.
- Words of interest from the story come from the children, mean something to them, and therefore can be learned more readily (Ashton-Warner, 1963).

- The children learn about word families, first at the level of initial letter similarity, and then when the word wall is developed with the highlighting of onset and rime.

Spelling

One concern for teachers of young children is that the use of the word wall might reduce the children's use of invented spellings. After all, if there are numerous words displayed, then the children have less need to go through the process of sounding out the word in order to determine how it might be represented in print. That serves as a reminder that the teacher needs to use the word wall with care and thought. The children's involvement with invented spellings is too precious to be lost.

Interestingly, invented spelling is one of the key links between whole language and phonic-based views of early reading development. Goodman (1990) indicates how children are active constructors of knowledge. The invented spelling of children not only tells us about what they know, it also shows how they are constructing literacy from an increasingly sophisticated understanding of print conventions. Adams (1990) from an alternative perspective also notes the value of invented spellings:

> In overview, classroom encouragement of invented spellings and independent writing from the start seems a promising approach towards the development of literacy skills. Beyond all that was mentioned above and whether the children are directing their efforts towards good descriptions or imaginative stories, this approach appears incomparable for purposes of developing their abilities to reflect on their own thoughts, to elaborate and organize their ideas, and to express themselves in print. (pp. 386–387)

The teacher will want to support young children in their understanding of print and in the production of words within writing. The word wall can support the children in those endeavors as it helps to create for each child a visual memory of some key and frequently used words that can then be written automatically and conventionally. However, the teacher will want to ensure that for much of the time, and with many words, the children are actively engaged in constructing the word themselves using their knowledge of letters and sounds. Initially, that leads to invented rather than conventional spellings. It also lays the foundations of literacy knowledge that will serve the children well in the future.

Knowledge of letters, phonics, and spelling are all developed from read-alouds and the associated literacy activities, such as writing, which arise naturally from those readings. Young children learn about print features because they are immersed in language and literacy. Teachers can support and guide that learning as they talk about print before and after the enjoyable read-alouds.

CHAPTER 4

Activities Based on the Read-Aloud

Some teachers use a read-aloud early in the day. For instance, Hart-Hewins and Wells (1990) often schedule the read-aloud time just before the children's work period. This allows the teachers to suggest activities that link the story with the children's play, writing, and art. Drawing and writing about a book helps children understand and think through the story. When teachers choose high-quality books, most children are inclined to follow the read-aloud by responding in some way, whether they engage in role-play, draw, write, make a book, construct a model, create and use a puppet, or learn a song. These forms of response will vary for each child, but some response is likely.

It is clear that a wide range of activities, or "enterprises" as Routman (1991) refers to them (p. 88), can be developed from stories that are read to children. However, it is essential that the stories remain paramount and the other activities and learning are derived naturally from them. Not every book should be linked into the work of the class. Nevertheless, the teacher should be aware of the activities that can be generated by each story, and consequently use the children's enthusiasm and enjoyment of the story as a guide to the activities that are provided or suggested.

For instance, prior to reading *Let's Go Home, Little Bear* (Waddell, 1991) to the class, a Grade 1 teacher considered possible avenues for development. She mapped those possible activities into a subject web (see Figure 10).

Subsequently, the teacher did not use all of these activities. Instead she used the children's interests to determine the direction of the follow-up. Nevertheless, the web reminded the teacher of possibilities as the children explored the story.

FIGURE 10
Subject Web for *Let's Go Home, Little Bear*

English
Story reading
Discuss pictures
Discuss story
Oral retelling
Writing own version
Alphabet book (word wall)
Sounds for letters
Nonfiction bear books
Other bear stories

Math
Explore big/little
Sizes
Measure own feet
Graph of feet sizes
Big/small sounds
Sorting

Art/Craft
Frieze of cold lands
Footprint patterns
Three-dimensional
    models
Cave paintings
Collages

Let's Go Home, Little Bear

Music
Loud and soft sounds
Moving to different sounds
Sing "The bear went over the mountain"
Make own instruments for sounds in book

Geography
Map of bear walk
Go on own walk - map
Cold lands of country
Cold lands of world
Animals of cold lands

Science
Sounds - wind, rain, water (natural)
            - car, planes, instruments (made)
Cold/hot - ice/water/steam (changes)
Exploring footprints
Bear characteristics

History
Dwellings - animal/
    human
Cave dwellings
Present homes
Heating and lighting

P.E./Dance
Move to sounds in book
(Heavy/light)

Following the Read-Aloud

Many teachers follow the read-aloud by supporting the children's explorations of the story in a variety of ways. The examples that follow come from different classrooms and age groups and discuss a range of stories.

Role-Play

Young children will quite naturally use the stories they have heard in their play activities in the classroom (Carter, 1999). Teachers can support the children's learning by linking a role-play area to a recent story, such as arranging a corner to resemble a cave after the class reads *Can't You Sleep, Little Bear?* (Waddell, 1988). The story begins,

> "Can't you sleep, Little Bear?"
> asked Big Bear, putting down his Bear Book
> (which was just getting to the interesting part) and
> padding over to the bed.
> "I'm scared," said Little Bear.
> "Why are you scared, Little Bear?" asked Big Bear.
> "I don't like the dark," said Little Bear.

During the role-play, the children can act out aspects of the story, and in this instance revisit their own concerns, such as a fear of the dark. And because this book contains positive literacy images as Big Bear reads a book, the teacher can place a small collection of books in the "cave" to support the play.

Hall and Robinson (1985) suggest that the use of storybooks with literacy-based images may contribute to children's understanding of reading and writing. However, it is the characters and events of the stories that provide such a strong basis for the children's play. As White (1954) indicates in relation to her daughter Carol's play at home, "How these children's books take hold and inhabit her mind!" (p. 164). Stories do indeed capture the children's minds, extend their imagination, and support their role-play activities.

The amount of adult involvement in the role-play can vary. It may be limited to the actual story reading, or it may involve preparing an area to reflect the setting of a book. In some classrooms, the level of teacher involvement and direction for role-play is even greater. Morado, Koenig, and Wilson (1999) report on their work with children in kindergarten through Grade 2 in which they brought together "literature, drama, music and movement" (p. 116). The children developed miniperformances from the basis of an initial reading of a story. The teachers guided the process through six 30-minute sessions during a 3-week period. The more formal aspects of this role-play included the creation of a script using the children's own words, the children's use of the scripts, and the performance that linked to a small audience of classmates, teachers, and family. Through this process, the children heard a story read a number of times, helped to produce the writing of the script, learned the words of the script, and demonstrated their literacy to the family. All this developed from the basis of play with stories.

Drawing and Writing

Children frequently enjoy having the opportunity to draw and write about story characters. In another classroom of first-grade children, the teacher chose *Four Fierce Kittens* (Dunbar, 1991) as a read-aloud. Some of the children responded with their own telling and writing of that story. The teacher included four of the key words on a word wall—*kittens*, *frighten*, *scare*, and *animals*—and the responses and writing were indicative of children with different levels of confidence with print. Figure 11 contains just one sentence: *one day fore kittens went to scare the sheep.* The sentence does not begin with a capital letter, although it does end with a period. The child used two of the displayed words, *kittens* and *scare*. In addition, six words are written conventionally. The one invented spelling—*fore*—is an appropriate representation for the word *four* although it is not spelled conventionally.

For another child, the writing was more extensive (see Figure 12). Here there is the conventional fairy tale opening of "Once upon a time...." There are four sentences, which are each marked by capital

---

FIGURE 11
Kitten Sentence

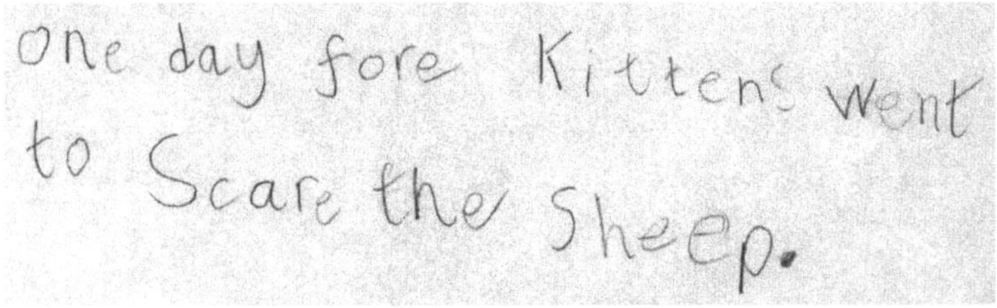

one day fore Kittens went to Scare the sheep.

FIGURE 12
Four Sentences About Kittens

Once upon a time There lived four Kittens They Were aSleep. It Was So Boring SO They Went to SCare the other animals on the farm.

letters and periods, although capital letters appear at other times too. All the words are spelled conventionally.

Both the children's responses include the main feature of the story, which is about kittens scaring other creatures on a farm. However, in the second piece of writing, the child was able to extend that idea and provide a reason for the kittens' behavior.

As the children write their own versions of a story, they may reveal which parts they found most important. For example, in Figure 13,

5-year-old John wrote a version of *Rosie's Walk* (Hutchins, 1987). In that story, a fox appears only in the illustrations; it plays no part in the words. However, John included the fox in his retelling, and explained in his final sentence that he enjoyed the story because the bag of flour fell on the fox.

One of the fascinating aspects of John's piece is the way he was confident enough to include *decided*, *sneaked*, and *stalking* in his writing. Other children will be far more restrained in their writing, although they may have fewer reversals and clearer handwriting than John produced.

If Rosie the hen can go for a walk, then the teacher and young children can also do so. (The opportunity for this varies from school to school according to the situation.) This extends the story and leads to other writing activities. When John's class went for a walk, the children talked with the adults about what they saw as they walked. When they returned to the classroom, the teacher gave them the opportunity to represent the walk with words and pictures. Michael wrote about some of what he had seen (see Figure 14).

FIGURE 13
John's Version of *Rosie's Walk*

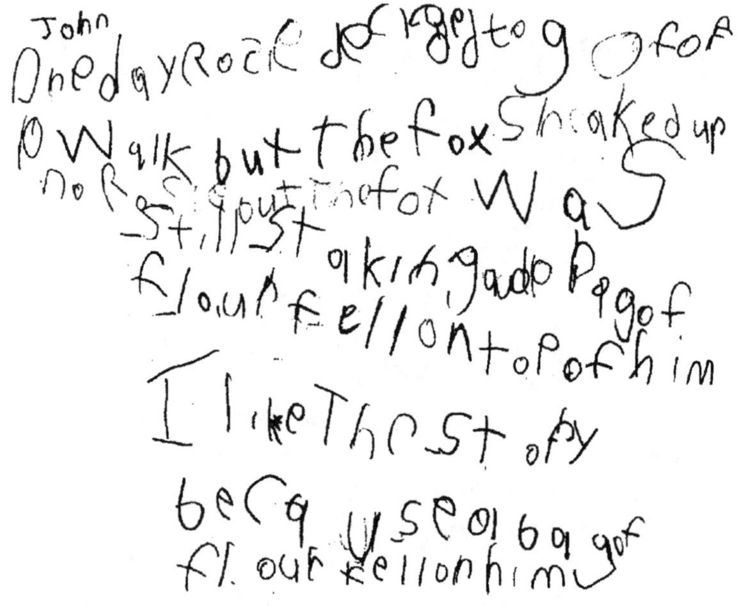

FIGURE 14
Michael's Writing After Class Walk

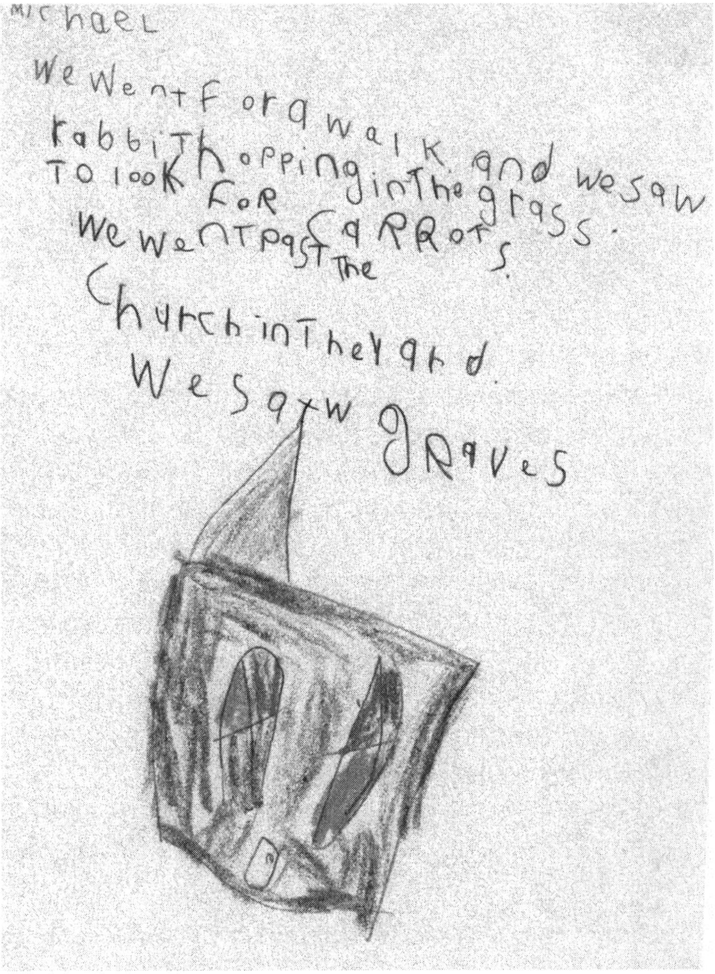

michael

We Went for a walk and we saw
rabbiT hopping in The grass.
TO look for caRRots.
we wenTpasT The
church inThe yard.
We saw graves

The two key features of Michael's writing are his imagination and his observation. The rabbits may have been hopping on the grass, but Michael was linking to other ideas when he suggested they were looking for carrots. We can only guess at why the graves appear as his second observation from all that he saw. He may already have begun to consider fundamental issues for humankind.

Making Books

Children love to be involved in making their own books. Those books can be constructed in a small group, with the whole class, or individually. Burman (1990) suggests that both class and individual book-making should be regular features of young children's classroom experience.

When Michael wrote about his walk, he produced a short piece of writing on his own. At the same time, he was also aware that it was going to contribute to a class book. The class book, titled *Our Walk*, linked to the story of *Rosie's Walk*. The teacher pasted the children's writing on the right-hand pages and neatly summarized their contributions on the left-hand pages. For example, opposite Michael's writing, she wrote, "We went past the church. In the yard we saw graves." The clear print on each left-hand page helped the children read the book for themselves when it was placed in the classroom library. They also recognized that the teacher had used their words. The children felt they had authored *Our Walk*, and those feelings created a sense of ownership.

The children might also contribute to a class book as part of a shared or interactive writing session as they re-create a story. (These collaborative writing activities are discussed in more detail in Chapter 6.) Again, the children will feel that they have authored the book. Although the individual contributions from the children will be less evident in the finished product of a shared writing, their efforts from an interactive writing session will be clear for all to see.

When the children produce class books in these ways, they complete the circle of reading-writing-reading. The read-aloud excites their interest and provides a basis for creating their own writing. Their writing forms a book for them and others to read. Then the collaborative texts help the class build a library of treasured books.

In addition to making class books, children also enjoy individual bookmaking. Burman (1990) suggests that one way to help children start writing is to ask what they know a lot about. From this discussion, the teacher can help the children create a brainstorming web that provides a plan for the writing. The class can also create a web about a book from a read-aloud. Each child can then draw and write about characters or other features of the book, re-create the story, or develop another story.

There are several ways to help children create individual books. For example, the teacher can staple the children's drawing and writing into book form. Alternately, each child can write in an eight-page booklet that Johnson (1998) describes as an "origami book" (p. 9).

The booklet provides a front cover and back cover with three double spreads of six pages inside. Those six pages, Johnson argues, are an ideal writing project planner. He suggests that when the six pages are seen as three spreads, the "fundamental story structure of beginning, middle and end fits it like a glove" (p. 8).

Children enjoy making and using these small books. It is immediately obvious to them that the task is manageable and that when they are done they will have their own books. As Routman (1991) indicates, these books become "a fantastic and favorite resource" (p. 90). The attraction of being an author and having ownership of a book encourages children to draw and write about the stories they enjoy in read-alouds.

Arts and Crafts

When children use a booklet to re-create their response to a story, they usually include some drawings. In an eight-page booklet, children typically enjoy creating a picture on each page, followed by a word, phrase, or sentence of description. Therefore, they are already linking art to literacy as a follow-up to a story.

At other times, the children enjoy creating larger pictures of the key characters or events of the story. When the classroom is organized so that children can paint at various times throughout the day, many children paint as a response to a story read-aloud. Morrow (1989) suggests that kindergarten classrooms should be set up to include an art center. Hart-Hewins and Wells (1999) also refer to a separate paint center, although they recognize that space restrictions might lead to having just one center. A range of paints and paper provide the basis for the children to explore their interest in the story.

The teacher can use the children's enthusiasm for representing aspects of the story in paint. Many kindergarten teachers create opportunities for children to create a collage of events from a story. Through this activity, the children are encouraged to paint, they work collaboratively, and they can discuss the best organization for the collage. Cloth, cardboard, foil, tissue paper, and other materials can be used to stick onto a three-dimensional collage. Throughout this activity, the children remain engrossed in the details of the story—which character to paint, which events to depict, and so forth. Therefore, while they are painting, the children are also engaged in literacy development.

Once the collage is completed and on display, the class can discuss what print might be included. For instance, if the collage represents aspects of *The Very Hungry Caterpillar*, the class might choose to include some of the words, phrases, and sentences from the story. Furthermore, the production of that writing for the collage display provides further opportunities for the teacher and children to work together on literacy. In the kindergarten classroom featured in Chapter 1, the class worked together to add print to their caterpillar collage:

Teacher:	That caterpillar is among all the strawberries. How many strawberries have we got?
Jamie:	Four.
Teacher:	We have. So what shall we write here?
Danny:	On...On Thursday he eated [sic] four strawberries.
Teacher:	He did. *On Thursday* *he ate through* *four strawberries,* *but*
Children:	*he was still* *hungry.*
Teacher:	So I'll write *On*. Who is going to help me?
Teresa:	*O* and *n*.
Teacher:	That's right: *On*.

This short excerpt shows how the children were involved in the production of some writing as they returned once more to the enjoyment of the story. Notice, too, how the teacher accepted Danny's contribution and then immediately provided a model of the actual words from the book. All the children know that "he was still hungry." And Teresa was able to help the teacher write the first word: *On*. Once the writing was completed, the class returned to the collage from time to time for shared reading, an extension of the read-aloud in which the entire class can see the text and focus on print features. (Shared reading is discussed in more detail in Chapter 5.)

In addition to painting, children enjoy constructing models as part of a story response. Often they will use boxes and other scrap material to aid their construction. Paper, glue, scissors, boxes, egg cartons, toothpicks, cotton balls, and other materials provide a good basis for the children to explore and construct. Dough or clay are also good mediums for children. Each opportunity to construct a model can extend the children's thinking about the story. Pahl (1999) argues that for some children, and perhaps especially some boys, model making is an important link to literacy. The main emphasis of her book was the preschool classroom, but she also notes how a second-grade child, Michael, became very involved in writing when the activity was related to a model he had just constructed. Many children will be thinking of a narrative—and developing their understanding of a text—as they paint and construct.

Making and Using Puppets

While making puppets is an extension of arts and crafts, it also creates very specific opportunities for linking to the story. The kindergarten class featured in Chapter 1 used stick puppets as part of a reading of *The Very Hungry Caterpillar*. The activity generated so much interest, the children also decided to make mouse puppets after the teacher read aloud another book by Carle, *Do You Want to Be My Friend?* (1991).

Powell and Hornsby (1998) describe how three children in a second-grade class created stick puppets following a reading of *Possum Magic* (Fox, 1983). They used the puppets as part of their own play activities, and wrote a script for their puppet play. Even younger children can plan a puppet play, and a few may be able to begin to construct a simple script.

One of the attractions of the stick puppet is that it is so easy to make. The child draws a picture of the character, cuts it out, and attaches it to a stick or rolled paper for the handle. Features of the setting or objects from the story—such as four strawberries—also can be drawn, cut out, and attached to a handle to become part of the story told by the young puppeteers.

There may also be occasions when children can create glove or finger puppets, or masks. In some cases, shy children are able to become more vocal when the glove, finger, or mask is the main object of attention. And, as the children act out or re-create the story, its words and rhythms remain in their thinking and become more firmly known.

Songs and Rhymes

Children enjoy singing songs and rhymes that relate to the topic of the book, and the activity increases their learning. Ruby Campbell (1998) provides another example of how a story provides for a wide variety of learning. In a preschool classroom, the teacher read *Barn on Fire* (Amery, 1989), a story about what appears to be a fire in a barn, but the smoke is actually from a picnic fire on the other side of the barn. The teacher introduced the following song:

> London's Burning,
> London's Burning.
> Fetch the engine,
> Fetch the engine.
> Fire, Fire,
> Fire, Fire.
> Pour on water,
> Pour on water.

Eventually, the class learned the song together with actions such as holding a hand to the mouth to call out "Fire, Fire" and pretending to "pour on water" with an imaginary bucket. As there was initially some confusion about using a bucket to pour on water, the teacher also told the children briefly about the subject of the song:

> Teacher: My song is about London a long time ago when the houses
>   were made of wood and they were very close together. There
>   were no telephones to get fire engines and they had to use
>   buckets to "pour on water." Shall we sing it again?
>   *London's Burning,*
>   *London's Burning....* (Campbell, 1998, p. 134)

At the end of the day, the children left the classroom telling the adults who had come to collect them all about the story, or singing the song to them.

As Campbell notes, this link with the parents is important. It ensures that some of the literacy learning from the classroom is developed further at home (Weinberger, Hannon, & Nutbrown, 1990). In some preschools and schools, a listing of days when parents are encouraged to visit the classroom creates opportunities for parents to work in the classroom alongside the children. These visits let parents witness the nature of the read-aloud. In other schools, the read-aloud is demonstrated and debated during parent-teacher meetings. The link enables the parents to share some of the children's excitement of the learning that has taken place during and following a read-aloud. And it means that many children are able to continue singing and taking part in other activities at home long after the read-aloud has taken place.

The read-aloud also leads into other reading activities. The wide range of possibilities is explored in the next chapter.

CHAPTER 5

Interactive Reading Activities

Shared Reading

In *The Foundations of Literacy*, Don Holdaway (1979) introduced and developed the important activity of *shared book experience*. In recent years this activity has become known as *shared reading* (Smith & Elley, 1994), but the nature of the activity remains. The adult demonstrates the reading process with a Big Book or with other print in an enlarged format, and the children contribute to the activity by reading some of the print, making comments, and asking questions. It is a literacy activity that is used frequently in classrooms with young children—and for good reason.

The important difference between read-alouds and shared reading relates to the visibility of the print. The print used for a shared reading is sufficiently large so that it can be "seen, shared and discussed" (Holdaway, 1979, p. 64). The book may be held or placed on a stand. Teachers should place themselves in a position that does not obscure the children's vision.

During shared reading, the teacher is likely to make more comments about the print and to draw from the children's comments and questions about the print. This replicates the one-on-one read-aloud experience the children may have at home with an adult, when they can see the print easily. In addition, shared reading provides additional opportunities for the class to discuss characters, events, and story meanings.

In an example of a shared reading as it was first developed, Holdaway (1979) describes the reading and the questions the teacher asks. The blanks indicate where the children joined in.

Teacher: *One day she met a frog.*   "Who is she talking to?"
          She said — — —:   "How many words?"

> *"Frog, frog,*
> *please play with me*   A repetitive section suitable for
> *I'm all by myself*   chiming in.
> *As you can see."*
>
> *"Yes," said the frog,*
> *"I will — — —,*   "What does she want him to do?"
> *We will play at j——."*   Perhaps discuss names begin-
>   ning with *j*.
>   (Holdaway, 1979, p. 69)

In this short example, the teacher encourages thinking about the text and the print. For instance, just as in a read-aloud, the children are encouraged to join in with the repetitive section of the story. Then the teacher's question "What does she want him to do?" prompts the children to consider the events of the story. The teacher may also use the story's letters and letter sounds to link the word *jumping* with children's names beginning with *j*. This helps them consider letters and sounds within the context of the story.

Slaughter (1992) also provides an extended discussion and examples of shared book experiences. Like Holdaway, she argues that the use of Big Books enables the classroom teacher to "simulate the bedtime story experience" (p. 16). Slaughter also notes a wide range of activities that could follow from the reading of the text, and indicates a number of simple but key practical points for the classroom teacher.

To select books for shared reading, teachers should use the same criteria as they do for read-aloud selection. Books should include the predictable features of repetition, rhyme, and rhythm (Rhodes, 1981). In some instances, a particularly appropriate book may not have been produced in Big Book format. In that case, the teacher may decide to create a Big Book from that text. In addition, other printed material may be produced for shared reading. Nursery rhymes, songs, poems, and notices can all be generated in large print for use in shared reading.

Shared reading also provides a good opportunity for the teacher to read from a range of nonfiction texts, including dictionaries (Goodwin & Redfern, 2000). As teachers read passages from science and social science texts, they can encourage the students to notice the use of layout, headings, numbered sections, bold print, contents, index, and glossary. Such discussions help young children understand the differences between narrative and informative texts. This understanding further supports the children's own reading and writing of different genres.

In another kindergarten classroom, the teacher selected the Big Book of *Rosie's Walk* (Hutchins, 1987) for shared reading. During the first reading, the emphasis was on the sheer enjoyment of the text. At the same time, the teacher very clearly followed the print with a pointer as she read. During the second reading, she talked about some of that print:

Teacher: Can you remember what this first page says?
            Rosie the

Children: *hen went for a walk*

Teacher: Yes. *Rosie the hen went for a walk.* So where does it say *hen*? You come and show me, Brian.
            [Brian points to the word *hen* with the pointer.]

Teacher: Yes, that's right. How many letters are there in *hen*?

Anna: Three.

Teacher: Yes, that's right. What are the letters?

Tina: *h-e-n.*

Teacher: Yes, *h-e-n.*

Later in this shared reading, the children commented on the other main character in the story:

Sam: It doesn't say *fox* anywhere.

Teacher: No, it doesn't, but we know the fox is in the story don't we?

Michelle: We can see the picture.

Teacher: Yes, that's right, the fox is always there. What is the first letter for *fox*?

Sam: *f*

Teacher: Yes, the letter *f*.

Jane: And it's got an *x*.

Teacher: It has, but there is another letter in between. I'll write *f* and *x*, but what else do we need for *fox*? [She places an emphasis on the *o*.]

With the children's assistance, the teacher continued to talk about the three letters of *fox*. This excerpt shows how the enjoyment of the story was followed by a consideration of the writing concerning the two main characters. Even though *fox* is not written in the text, it became a word of interest.

Rosie's Walk is also featured in Slaughter's (1992) work with a first-grade class. After the teacher read the story, the class spent a week engaged in a variety of activities based on the text. In terms of print features, the letters *R* and *H* formed a major focus. On the Tuesday, a group of children looked through the book to find words beginning with *R* or *H*. Then they determined which children in the class had names that started with one of those letters. The class worked on charts of words that begin with each letter. In addition to the words they found in *Rosie's Walk*, the children added other words beginning with those letters. In all, they produced 11 words for each chart. In addition, they followed the story by writing, making puppets, and listening to other stories by Pat Hutchins.

Teachers do not have to choose between a read-aloud and shared reading. Both have a part to play in children's literacy development. The daily read-aloud is about the story and sometimes the activities that flow naturally from it and from the children's interest in the story. The shared reading allows for a more detailed consideration of the print, although many activities also can flow from this reading. In both instances, the teacher will be aware that the enjoyment of the text is important. The nature of these literacy activities must not be allowed to become so analytic that the children lose interest in the stories, books, and reading.

Sustained Silent Reading

Sustained Silent Reading (SSR) is a natural activity to follow the read-aloud. When young children are given the opportunity to engage in SSR, it gives them a chance to act out reading-like behaviors. It also provides them with the opportunity to read a well-loved read-aloud book on their own, using the model that has been provided by the adult through numerous read-alouds and shared readings. For some this activity may not yet be silent. The youngest children will vocalize as they read, and some children will need to comment on a picture or the relationship of the text to their own life. However, these children are moving toward silent reading individually.

In many classrooms, other acronyms have been used to describe SSR. Among the more frequently used are Sustained Quiet Un-Interrupted Reading Time (SQUIRT) and Drop Everything and Read (DEAR). In one Grade 1 classroom, the children had an allocated time for BE A Reader (BEAR). Capitalizing on this title, the teacher encouraged an exploration of books about bears. Pictures, models, toys, and the children's own writing about Winnie the Pooh, Paddington, and other bears added to the excitement and interest in this period of reading.

Typically, teachers use a short daily period for SSR. For ease of organization, this usually occurs immediately before or after a recess. Trelease (1995) describes a classroom where the children selected a book before going to lunch and left it on their desk. Then the first 10 minutes after lunch provided a time for SSR. The teacher noted that this short period of reading totals almost an hour of concentrated reading each week.

The children select their own books during this period of reading, and there is no requirement for the children to report on their reading. Trelease (1995) stresses that the teacher or other adults in the room must also read during this time, which provides a strong model of reading for the children. However, Hart-Hewins and Wells (1990) suggest that the teacher may want to use SSR as a time to hold individual reading conferences. Campbell and Scrivens (1995) consider those differing views and note that the best course of action might depend on the overall ethos of the classroom. In classrooms where there is a dynamic literacy program in place, with an enthusiastic teacher who supports the literacy activities, then modeling during SSR is not essential. When there is less emphasis on literacy, modeling appears to be required to keep the children reading. The real issue may be to ensure that SSR is organized so that the young children are aware of the process of this worthwhile activity.

Individual Reading

The individual reading activity can be viewed in a number of ways. First, it might be considered as a one-to-one interaction with the adult reading to the child. This type of interaction is especially important for children who have not had the opportunity to be part of read-alouds before entering school, even when there are daily read-alouds and shared reading in the classroom. These individual read-alouds allow the teacher or other adult to ensure that the child is involved in the story, is making contributions, and is beginning to pick up on print features.

Second, the individual reading activity can be seen as a time for individual reading conferences. During these conferences, especially in the later grades, it is the child who might read to the teacher. Holdaway (1979) argues that the shared book experience leads to individual reading as a child rereads a book previously read by the teacher. After the child's reading, the adult and child can discuss the content and consider various aspects of print.

To see how this works, I studied 6-year-old Leah's individual reading of *Good-Night Owl* (Hutchins, 1972) with her Grade 1 teacher (Campbell, 1990, pp. 47–53). In the following transcript, the original text appears in parentheses after her miscues:

Leah: *The starlings chittered,*
            tweet-tweet (twit-twit) tweet-tweet (twit-twit)
            and owl tried to sleep.
            The jays screamed,
            ark ark,
            and owl tried to sleep.
            The cuckoo croaked (called)
Teacher: *The cuckoo*
Leah: *called*

Leah was able to read substantial amounts of this book, partly because of her memory of the text, and also because she paid attention to the print. The teacher had to determine when to mediate in the reading. She ignored the miscue of *tweet-tweet* (*twit-twit*), but she did support Leah's reading when the child read *croaked* for *called*. Using the simple strategy of starting the sentence again, the teacher gave Leah time to reflect, to consider the word in context, and to self-correct.

Later, when the entire book had been read, the teacher developed a dialogue with Leah that emphasized meaning:

Teacher: Why couldn't he sleep?
Leah: Because they were all making a noise.

Teacher:	Why do you think they were all making a noise? Mmh?
Leah:	Because it's still-umh...
Teacher:	In when?
Leah:	Because it's not night yet.
Teacher:	It isn't night time. And what do owls do at night time?
Leah:	They—They don't—umh—They don't sleep in night and they wake up....

It was evident that Leah knew about the story even though some of her attempts at an explanation were hesitant. Throughout the individual reading, the child was able to achieve a sustained involvement with the text, with support available from the teacher. Individual reading activities build children's confidence and enable them to behave like readers.

Buddy Reading

Everyday classroom demands limit the time available for the teacher and other adults to work alongside a young child with a book. Therefore, in a number of schools, schemes such as buddy reading are being initiated (Cunningham & Allington, 1999). This activity involves pairing an older child, perhaps a fourth or fifth grader, with a younger child. Once a week, the older child goes to another classroom to read a book with the younger child.

There are a number of benefits to such an activity. First, the older child must practice reading the picture book to ensure that it is read well for the younger child. For some 9- and 10-year-olds, that practice can be important. As Cunningham and Allington indicate, it "legitimizes the reading and rereading of very easy books" (p. 38). Further, the important teaching role helps the older children with their own reading development, and it does much for their self-esteem. At the same time, the younger buddies benefit from the interactive experience of the read-aloud.

In addition, the buddy system gives the younger children positive role models. In particular, young boys may benefit from the presence of successful male readers, especially because many classrooms for young children are staffed by females. As Cunningham and Allington remind us, "most elementary teachers are women and...most poor readers are boys" (p. 37). Some schools even extend buddy reading to include adults from the community as readers to work alongside the child with a book.

Paired Reading

In addition to buddy reading, the children can work together in their own classroom to read a book. So paired reading (also called *partner reading*) can operate with two 5-year-old kindergarten students or two 6-year-old Grade 1 children helping each other to read a book. Cunningham and Allington (1999) suggest that the teacher can designate a number of different activities to create some variety for paired reading:

> During a "take turn day," the two children read alternate pages. They also help each other as the need arises. This is likely to be the most frequently used form of paired reading; the children soon become familiar with the approach and are able to use it successfully.

> An "ask question day" requires both children to read each page silently and ask each other a question about the text before proceeding. In some first- and second-grade classrooms, the teacher may encourage the children to ask questions about features of the print on one day and to encourage a greater attention to the story content on another day.

> Another day might be used as a "sticky note day." The teacher gives the children a limited number of sticky notes to mark what interests them. Alternately, the children can concentrate on what they consider to be important or aspects they find confusing.

> A "you decide day" permits the children to make their own decision as to how they will operate the paired reading on that day.

As Cunningham and Allington note, these different forms of paired reading create variety, encourage the children to engage in both silent and oral reading, and lead them to reflect on what they have read.

Guided Reading

In a typical guided reading time, the teacher will work with a small group of children. Six is often suggested as an ideal size for a group. All the children will have a copy of a book they can enjoy and manage. With younger children, the management of the text is supported when the book has been read aloud previously to the class. Mooney (1990) indicates that the purpose of guided reading is to "develop independent readers who question, consider alternatives, and make informed choices as they seek meaning" (p. 47). She argues that the teacher role during this literacy activity is to guide the children to predict as they read, to sample the features of print necessary to confirm expectations, to confirm that meaning has been maintained, and to self-correct using other strategies when necessary to regain meaning.

The teacher then guides the children with their reading of a specific text, but this is done in a way that helps the children to read other texts independently in the future. Fountas and Pinnell (1996) provide very detailed information on this activity that many teachers find useful. Chomsky-Higgins (1998) provides an example in which she selects a book that enables the children to be successful but offers some challenges. If the children have not encountered the story previously, she tells them the title, and together they go through the book to get an idea of the meaning. She asks the children to read a few specific words at this time. After this supportive introduction, the children read the book aloud as she moves around the group to listen in and guide when necessary. A brief discussion may follow that reading.

Literature Circles

As Short (1999) notes, young children also need reading to help them make sense of life. She argues that children should not have to wait until they've developed extended reading strategies to find out that reading involves critique and inquiry. In literature circles, as in guided reading, the teacher works with a small group of children who each have copies of the same book. During literature circles, however, the primary interest centers on thinking about the story and discussing its aspects.

When quality picture books are read aloud, children will want to discuss what they see and hear. Roser and Martinez (1995) demonstrate that young children are keen to express their thoughts and feelings about the books that are read to them or that they have read in small groups. Initially, the teacher will have to prompt and guide the children, but eventually the children will provide comments with very little guidance.

The children's participation in literature circles is not surprising, because even younger children at home respond reflectively to stories that have been read aloud. For instance, I read *The Very Lonely Firefly* (Carle,

1995) to my granddaughter Alice when she was 3 years, 11 months old, and she immediately requested a repeat reading. However, within a few pages of that second reading, as the lonely firefly searches for other fireflies, Alice interrupted me to comment on the story: "It will find the other fireflies on the last page. Then it won't be lonely anymore."

The last page, with its illustrations of flashing lights, is a particular attraction of this book. Alice returned to her theme when we reached the final page. She said at once, "There's all its friends" (Campbell, 1999, pp. 89–90). Both comments show Alice's involvement with the story and her empathy for the firefly as it searched for others.

Teachers can encourage the children's responses to reading at home and in the classroom as they read aloud to children. The responses can then be developed further in literature circles as the children progress through the primary years.

The children's learning from read-alouds provides a strong footing for their work during other interactive reading activities. In addition, as Chapter 1 showed, read-alouds can also serve as the foundation for interactive writing activities. This subject is covered in more detail in Chapter 6.

Interactive Writing Activities

Just as teachers use Big Books to point out print features, they can write in front of the class to help the children become better writers. During shared writing (Cambourne, 1988), the teacher talks about the piece as it's developed to make the children aware of the writing process. Additional activities such as interactive writing, guided writing, and writing conferences also require the children's involvement as they contribute to the writing—or share their own—by considering, thoughts, sentences, words, and letters.

Shared Writing

The stories, songs, poems, and rhymes that the children already know provide a good starting point for shared writing. To see how this works, I studied a preschool class in which the teacher used the popular nursery rhyme of Humpty Dumpty to create a brief shared writing time with the children (Campbell, 1996, pp. 51–52). The class had talked about the rhyme and had sung it frequently. As the teacher wrote in front of the children on a large sheet of paper, she encouraged them to provide the words:

Teacher:	So if I write
	Humpty Dumpty
	Now, what comes next?
Children:	*sat on a wall*
Teacher:	I'll write
	sat on a...
Children:	*wall*
Teacher:	*wall.*
	There we are.

Humpty Dumpty
Teacher with children: *sat on a wall.*
Teacher: Now
               Humpty
Children: *Dumpty*
               had a great fall.

In this simple example, the children recited the rhyme and the teacher attempted to keep up with their pace. Her goal was to support the children in their understanding of the writing process and the link between words spoken and words presented in print. She encouraged the children's contributions by asking questions such as "Now, what comes next?" and by using careful intonation and pausing such as "sat on a...."

At times, this shared writing activity also included shared reading. After the first sentence was written, the teacher pointed to the words and recited them with the children. When the activity was complete, the teacher placed the printed rhyme on the classroom wall beside other rhyme sheets that had been created during shared writing. Throughout the year, the class used the sheets to recite the rhymes while the teacher pointed to the words.

With kindergarten children, the teacher usually spends more time considering each word as it is written. The teacher might comment on letters and letter sounds, and make links between the first letter of some words and the first letter of other words the children know.

Geekie, Cambourne, and Fitzsimmons (1999) note that in one kindergarten classroom, the teacher followed a structure they describe as follows:

i)   Making a clear statement about what is going to be written.
ii) Identifying each word in succession.
iii) Either
    a. recalling the identified word from memory
    b. finding it in the print environment of the classroom and copying it
    c. segmenting it into phonemes and making sound-symbol matches
iv) Re-reading the developing text in order to remember what has already been written and what remains to be written. (p. 40)

The teacher used what was termed "blackboard stories"—stories developed with the children—to link to other print in the classroom, including the word wall. A regular use of the activity enabled the children gradually to write stories on their own.

Anderson (1995) adopted a different strategy in a Grade 1 and 2 mixed classroom with 6- and 7-year-old children. To encourage the children to think about choices when writing, she selected a text they knew and loved—*The Very Hungry Caterpillar*—and reprinted the story in large text for all the children to see. Then she asked them to consider whether they would have used the same words and phrases as Eric Carle. A great deal of discussion ensued as the children changed aspects of the story. The start of the story became

> One dark cloudy night a tiny speckled egg lay on a leaf.
> One bright Saturday morning the warm sun came up and—crack!—out
>   of the egg came a tiny and very hungry caterpillar.
> She scrambled about to look for some food.
> On Sunday she ate through one nice ripe apple. But she was still hungry.
> On Monday she ate through two red shiny apples, but she was still hungry.
> On Tuesday she ate through three squidgy plums, but she was still hungry.
>   (p. 48)

Each of the redrafts involved a discussion, which meant that the children were talking about meaning, sentences, phrases, words, and letters. And because it seemed natural to do so, the teacher found herself using terms such as *adjective, pronoun, noun,* and *verb.* At one point, even the notion of tense in story writing became part of the discussion.

As the example indicates, the caterpillar became "she" rather than "he." Starting with a Saturday changed the sequence of the days of the week. The class also added some adjectives to each of the fruits. For a while the children played with alliterations, debating the use of "plump purple plums" before settling for their own word: *squidgy.* The teacher typed the revised text on the computer, printed it, and placed it into a book format for the class library. It became one of the most frequently read and borrowed books.

Anderson also worked with another group of children to rewrite *The Very Hungry Caterpillar.* However, after engaging in shared writing, these children wrote their own pieces. A child named Gillian decided to shorten the text and to start with a more conventional beginning. She transformed the story to read as follows:

Once upon a time it was a dark frosty night and
One Saterday morning the hot sun came up and the egg started to hatch.
A little and very hungry caterpillar came out
She went to find some food.
On Sunday she ate through 5 tomatoes but she was not hungrey
    Anymore.
On Monday she ate through one leaf but she had a tumy ake
On Tuesday she was a beautiful butterfly. (Anderson, 1995, p. 52)

Although Gillian ended up with a shorter story than the original, she had worked hard to create her own piece of writing. The initial shared writing work with the class and the teacher supported her independent writing.

Well-known stories can be used as the basis for other shared writing experiences. Johnson and Louis (1985) suggest the writing of literary letters as a means of creating genuine opportunities for writing. In particular, they note that children could create their own letters to a character in a familiar story, such as Mike from *Mike Mulligan and His Steam Shovel* (Burton, 1977), and the teacher could respond to them. In a classroom where *The Very Hungry Caterpillar* has been read, the teacher might choose to respond to a letter such as the one shown in Figure 15, which was written by a second-grade child.

In particular, the teacher might wish to pick up on the scientific inquiry in the last sentence: "How long are you going to stay in your cocoon?"

In an example drawn from work with older primary children, Johnson and Louis also indicate that the class could work together to compose such a letter, with the teacher leading a discussion with the children and scribing their thoughts. According to the class's needs at that time, the teacher can place an emphasis on different features of the writing process. Mainly the emphasis will be on meaning, but the teacher may also draw the class's attention to the print features of the letters, words, phrases, and sentences that the children select.

Interactive Writing

McCarrier, Pinnell, and Fountas (1999) suggest that while shared writing is an important literacy activity for young children, it's possible

FIGURE 15
Letter Written by a Second-Grade Child

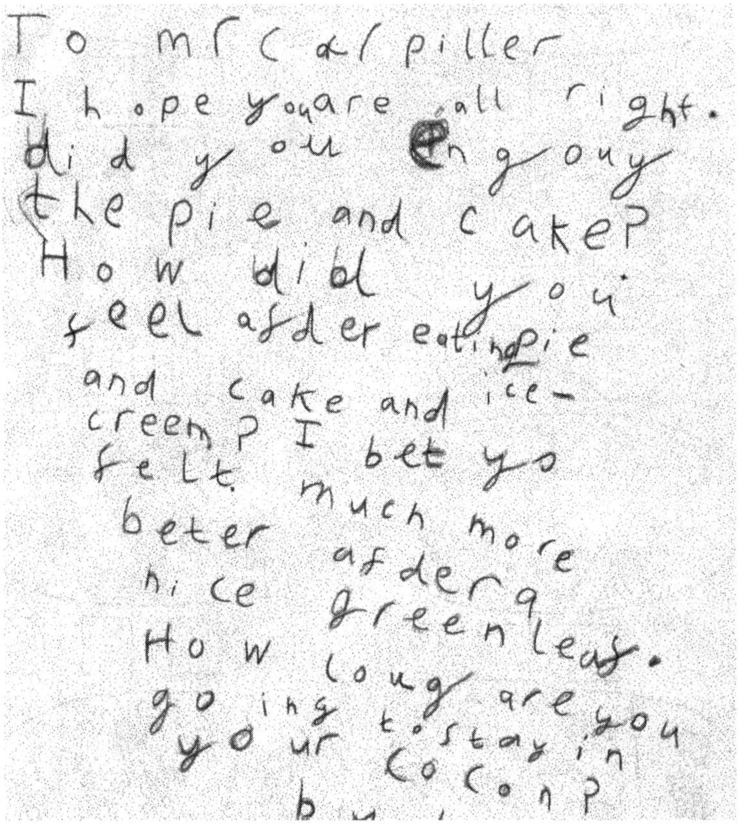

To mrcalpiller
I hope youare all right.
did you Engouy
the pie and cakeP
How did you
feel afder eatinpie
and cake and ice-
creem? I bet yo
felt. much more
beter
nice afdera
How greenleas.
going are you
your tostayin
bu con?

to involve the children even further in a process they call *interactive writing*. Interactive writing proceeds like shared writing, but the children take turns writing the words in front of the class, supported and guided by the teacher. The teacher also writes some of the words as part of the guidance and support that is provided.

As McCarrier, Pinnell, and Fountas note, "sharing the pen is not simply a ritual"; instead, each time the child writes with the pen in front of the class, there is an instructional value (p. 21). The authors argue that interactive writing works well for children from a range of linguistic backgrounds and "for those transitioning into English literacy" (p. xvi). It does so because the children are actively engaged in the writing.

The authors also note that the main value of writing activities lies in the process, not the end product. Interactive writing provides an excellent opportunity for teachers to determine the children's learning needs and then plan an activity for the whole class or a small group. In both of these modes, the conversation about the writing topic is continuous. The teacher should also discuss the composing process, the conventions of writing, and interesting features of words. For example, if the class was working with the Humpty Dumpty rhyme, the teacher might want to ensure that the rime unit of *all*, *wall*, and *fall* became a central feature of discussion.

In one example from the many provided by McCarrier, Pinnell, and Fountas (1999), a read-aloud of *Pancakes, Pancakes* (Carle, 1990) stimulated the writing in the classroom. The book linked well with the class's study of food and nutrition, and Eric Carle was one of the children's favorite authors. During interactive writing, the class produced a list of pancake ingredients, a list of favorite pancake toppings, and a recipe for making pancakes. Each of these pieces of writing required the children to think and talk about writing, as well as to help in the process as they shared the pen.

Guided Writing

Like guided reading, in guided writing the teacher works with a small group of four to eight children. Six is often seen as the optimum number. The guided writing time is most often used either as a group shared writing enterprise, in which the teacher and children work collaboratively on a piece of writing, or as a minilesson, in which the teacher gathers together a small group of children with similar needs to work on a particular feature of writing.

When guided writing is used as a collaborative writing experience, it might also be based on a similar interest or need. For example, the group may decide to write a letter to a character in a story. During this writing, the teacher can place an emphasis on both meaning and form. And because the group is small, each child can provide more input and remain involved throughout the session. Throughout the session, the collaborative writing concentrates on the production of the content, but features of print are also discussed.

Graves (1994) describes the beginning of the writing in one kindergarten classroom:

Teacher: What do I want to say? Let's see.
"Billy and I go for walks."
Help me.
B...il...ly (She says the word very slowly)
Help me with the first sound "B."
What letter do I write here?
Brendan: B. I've got that one in my own name. It's easy. (p. 49)

In this example, aspects of print are discussed. Like many other children in kindergarten, Brendan is able to use the knowledge of his forename to help in producing other writing.

As a minilesson, guided writing provides small groups of children with a concentrated time to consider some small aspect of writing conventions. The objective of the short lesson may involve thinking about letters and sounds, punctuation, vocabulary, or spelling. For instance, a teacher working with a small group of first-grade children wanted to remind them of sentence conventions. First she looked at each sentence of a short book with the children, and they talked about the uppercase letters and punctuation. Then they read a piece of classroom print developed from a shared writing, again concentrating on the uppercase letters and punctuation. Finally, the children moved on to independent writing, and the teacher confirmed their use of an initial capital letter and sentence ending. Although the minilesson in guided writing is brief, it can support children's literacy development, especially when it can be timed by the teacher to meet their needs.

Writing Conferences

Children write in a variety of formats as they respond to stories. They might create a drawing accompanied by writing or make their own book. One-on-one writing conferences (Calkins, 1983) are particularly useful if they occur immediately after the child has finished writing, so the writing is still at the forefront of the child's mind. Furthermore, focusing on just one aspect of writing can lead the child to an increased understanding of that feature.

For example, in one classroom, the teacher chose the story *It's My Birthday* (Oxenbury, 1993) for a read-aloud. The central theme involves making a cake, and a number of animals work together to make this possible. For instance, the second page of the book reads:

"It's my birthday and
I'm going to make a cake.
I need some eggs."
"I'll get you some eggs,"
Said the chicken.

After several readings of this story, some children decided to make their own recipe books. Five-year-old Kate wrote about making a fruitcake (see Figure 16). She was clearly in charge of her writing, even though there are a number of invented spellings and a mixture of uppercase and lowercase letters throughout her recipe.

After Kate finished writing, she met with the teacher for a writing conference. During that meeting, the teacher acknowledged the value of the writing and talked to Kate about one of the words that was written unconventionally:

Teacher: I think this would make a great fruitcake. You've done well with your writing.

FIGURE 16
Kate's Fruitcake Recipe

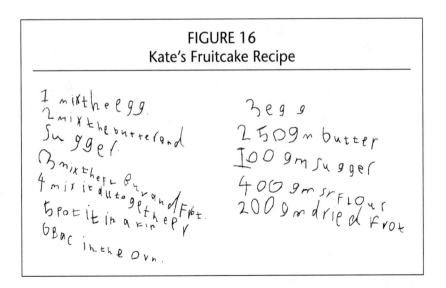

And to finish we have to...[She points to *6- Bac in the ovn*]

Kate: Bake in the oven.

Teacher: That's right. When we write *bake* it is *b-a-k-e*. It is just like *cake*.

Kate: *C-a-k-e*.

Teacher: I know another one that begins with *m*.

Kate: *Make*.

Teacher: That's right, *make*.

Kate: *M-a-k-e*.

Teacher: Good girl, that's how to write *make*. Well done, Kate; it's a lovely recipe.

Kate: *Take* is one as well.

Teacher: It is, isn't it?

The teacher helped Kate consider the word *bake*. Then they discussed other rime words in the *-ake* family. Interestingly, although the teacher was ready to finish the conference, Kate was in full swing and suggested another word: *take*. The conference may have been short, but it was personal. Therefore, there was a good chance that Kate would recall those *-ake* words in the future and write others like it—such as *lake* and *rake*—by analogy (Goswami & Bryant, 1990).

Read-alouds can lead the children into a variety of interactive writing activities. On some occasions, the teacher leads the children in this direction. Oftentimes the children want to explore further the story they have just heard, such as when the children decided to create recipe books after hearing *It's My Birthday*. The next chapter discusses how the read-aloud may also lead in other directions.

CHAPTER 7

Interactive Math, Science, and Social Studies Activities

Read-alouds also provide a link into other subject areas. Some stories inevitably bring other curriculum areas to the children's attention as they ask a variety of questions related to the story. These questions frequently lead to discussions about aspects of content areas such as mathematics, science, and social studies.

Mathematics

Chapter 1 described how *The Very Hungry Caterpillar* led the kindergarten children to the exploration of some aspects of mathematics and science. The children encountered the sequence of numbers 1 to 5 as the caterpillar consumed the apple, pears, plums, strawberries, and oranges. For most children, the sequence became firmly established, and they began to recognize the quantities of 1 to 5. As the children drew pictures of the five fruits and labeled them or created their own list of five different fruits, their understanding of numbers was established more firmly. In addition, the children enjoyed drawing other pictures of the caterpillar, especially recapturing the bold face, and their interest led to other mathematics. The teacher encouraged the children to measure the length of their drawn caterpillar with math cubes. The counting of those cubes involved numbers up to 14.

Many storybooks have mathematical features that the teacher can emphasize or that the teacher can follow up as the children begin to talk about that feature. For instance, in *Hairy Maclary from Donaldson's Dairy* (Dodd, 1983), each of the dogs, as they join the pack, can be seen coming from their house. Those houses are numbered 86, 84, 82. In one kindergarten classroom, the children noticed those numbers in the illustrations. Then they wanted to tell about the number on their houses. The children and the teacher asked a range of questions, such as "Which is the largest number?" The class then proceeded to create a collage of the "roads where we live," with the numbers painted on each house. In this instance, the teacher had planned none of these activities; the children's interests led the class to follow the mathematical theme. The children were excited by the attention given to the numbers in the story and the numbers on their own houses. They learned from that excitement and their concentration on "big numbers."

If the teacher wishes, it is possible to collect a number of books that are written with a mathematical theme in mind. For instance, *One Tiger Growls* (Wadsworth, 1999) provides a sequence from 1 to 20 as various animals and their sounds are presented. In this case, the sequence of 1 to 20 can be learned, or previous learning of 1 to 20 can be consolidated, with an enjoyable read-aloud.

Science

In the kindergarten classroom presented in Chapter 1, the children also explored aspects of science after hearing *The Very Hungry Caterpillar*. The life cycle of the butterfly became part of their knowledge base simply from the reading and rereading of the story. In that classroom, the teacher added a song that reminded the children of the life cycle. Importantly, as the children sang the song, they recognized that the life cycle could "go on forever." The story also led to an interest in what other animals eat. Then the class explored which foods are nutritious and which are not. It is not difficult to see how *The Very Hungry Caterpillar* led the children to think about these interests and therefore about aspects of science.

The story of the animals and the water hole in *Sniff-Snuff-Snap!* (Dodd, 1995) also creates scientific interests for young children. The sequence or cycle of rain and evaporation are part of the story that intrigues children. Then there is the role of the animals that are sustained by the water from the water hole in the otherwise arid countryside. This leads children to ask questions not only about the water supply within the story, but also about the water supply in their own lives.

Social Studies

A story like *Sniff-Snuff-Snap!* can also lead into other areas of the curriculum. What is it like in a country such as the one shown in this story? Discussions about desert lands often arise from stories such as *Sniff-Snuff-Snap!* An interest in geography may start from other stories, too. *Possum Magic* (Fox, 1983) contains a map of Australia that indicates the route taken by the two possums. The possums' journey and the "people food" they eat capture the attention, feelings, and minds of young children, and many children then want to learn more about Australia, the animals that live there, and the foods mentioned in the story. Creating a collage of the unique animals of Australia is an obvious extension from hearing this story. After all, the possum, koala, wombat, kangaroo, and duck-billed platypus do intrigue young children. Mem Fox's other books also include *Koala Lou* (1988) and *Wombat Divine* (1995). These books add to the children's knowledge and—most important—are stories they will love.

There are no maps in the story of *Rosie's Walk* (Hutchins, 1987), but Rosie creates a trail that can be mapped by children as they follow her path through the farmyard. A wall collage of Rosie's journey helps young children envision the story and begin to understand the nature of maps. When the children are captivated by the story, the teacher may decide to take them on walks in the local environment and then create maps of that walk. Other possibilities exist too. Children enjoy creating a map of their route to school. In this case the geography is local, rather than worldwide, which helps children understand their own environment.

The simple story of *When I Was Little Like You* (Walsh, 1997) also links to other curriculum areas. In this story, a little girl named Rosie talks with her grandmother and shows her various sights such as a train and an ice-cream van. In each instance, the grandmother indicates, "When I was little like you it used to be different," and then tells how it used to be when she was young. The historical changes over two generations are the most important features of the story, although relationships also play an important role. The story captures the children's interest in how life used to be long ago, and stimulates an interest in history. Often, the class can link interests from this story to family and community histories. Inspired by this story, children can explore how things used to be when the parents of their parents were young.

Stories can also be a useful means of introducing young children to history. Hoodless (1998) devotes a complete book to history and English in the primary grades in order to explore the vast number of connections that can be made. In addition, the children may link a classroom story to a theme that is already being pursued. For instance, in one case study of kindergarten children in England, Hoodless notes that after enjoying *The Three Billy Goats Gruff*, the children made a connection with the existing theme on Sir Robert Peel and the police. In this case, they decided to use the role-play area, which was already arranged as a Victorian police station, to create and hang "wanted posters" of the troll.

Wendy Hood (1994) shows how one teacher linked read-alouds and social studies themes with a class of Grade 3 children from a range of ethnic backgrounds. The children began by trying to find information about Native Americans. Over a period of weeks, this research led them in a number of different directions. They pursued such questions as "Where did they live? Where do they live now? What holidays do they celebrate?" Their findings also raised questions about slavery. In order to develop the children's understanding of these issues, the teacher read aloud a number of nonfiction texts, which helped the children extend their knowledge of the theme. At the same time, they also learned more about the organization of nonfiction books.

In this chapter, only a few storybooks have been used to demonstrate the links that can be made between read-alouds or shared readings and other curriculum areas. However, a resourceful teacher of young children can soon build a repertoire of books with links across the curriculum. Slaughter (1993) suggests a number of titles of children's books that can lead into mathematics, science, and social studies, as well as art and music. Children's learning is enhanced when they are given time to explore those interests, and their explorations lead to more reading and writing. The Afterword takes a final look at how the read-aloud itself plays an important part in young children's literacy development.

Afterword

Read-alouds are enjoyable and instructive. Every teacher of young children can name a story that has captivated the children. In one classroom, the children enjoyed *Hairy Maclary from Donaldson's Dairy* (Dodd, 1983). As noted earlier, the main characters, all dogs, include the following:

> Schnitzel von Krumm
> with a very low tum,
> Bitzer Maloney
> all skinny and bony,
> Muffin McLay
> like a bundle of hay,
> Bottomley Potts
> covered in spots,
> Hercules Morse
> as big as a horse
> and Hairy Maclary
> from Donaldson's dairy.

As the dog's adventure unfolded, the children remained excited. After the first story read-aloud was completed, the request for multiple readings came from more than one child. Because the characters are so lovable, young children want to return again and again to this story. As those rereadings take place, they learn more each time.

Fortunately for the children, there are other stories about Hairy Maclary and other key characters to enjoy. In one kindergarten classroom, the 5-year-old children became involved in a form of author study as they listened to, discussed, commented on, and followed the books by this one author.

The enjoyment children receive from read-alouds sparks their desire to read for themselves in a way that the worksheet can never emulate.

In addition, these books—and the thousands of other delightful books available for read-alouds—provide the foundation for a great deal of literacy learning as the children follow their interests by drawing, writing, painting, making puppets, acting, reciting, and moving on to other areas of the curriculum. The children also develop their phonic knowledge from meaningful contexts.

The characters from stories also reappear as they become part of the children's imaginative play. Chambers (1995) tells vividly about the child who had Little Red Riding Hood as an escort, in her imagination, to walk alone along a poorly lit path. The characters from children's stories become the children's friends. In addition, words, phrases, and sentences transfer from the stories into their language.

Each chapter in this book has emphasized how much literacy learning can follow from a well-prepared and enthusiastic read-aloud. No wonder then that so many teachers recognize the benefits of the read-aloud with young children.

References

Adams, M.J. (1990). *Beginning to read: Thinking and learning about print.* Cambridge, MA: MIT Press.

Anderson, H. (1995). About as big as the library: Using quality texts in the development of children as readers and writers. In E. Bearne (Ed.), *Great expectations* (pp. 43–56). London: Cassell.

Ashton-Warner, S. (1963). *Teacher.* London: Secker and Warburg.

Baghban, M. (1984). *Our daughter learns to read and write.* Newark, DE: International Reading Association.

Bettleheim, B., & Zelan, K. (1981). *On learning to read.* London: Penguin.

Bissex, G. (1980). *GNYS AT WRK: A child learns to read and write.* Cambridge, MA: Harvard University Press.

Bruner, J. (1968). Two modes of thought. In J. Mercer (Ed.), *Language and literacy from an educational perspective* (Vol. I, pp. 99–112). Milton Keynes, UK: Open University Press.

Burman, C. (1990). Organizing for reading 3–7. In B. Wade (Ed.), *Reading for real* (pp. 37–59). Buckingham, UK: Open University Press.

Butler, D. (1998). *Babies need books: Sharing the joy of books with children from birth to six* (Rev. ed.). Portsmouth, NH: Heinemann.

Calkins, L.M. (1983). *Lessons from a child: On the teaching and learning of writing.* Portsmouth, NH: Heinemann.

Cambourne, B. (1988). *The whole story: Natural learning and the acquisition of literacy in the classroom.* Sydney, Australia: Ashton Scholastic.

Campbell, R. (1990). *Reading together.* Buckingham, UK: Open University Press.

Campbell, R. (1992). *Reading real books.* Buckingham, UK: Open University Press.

Campbell, R. (1996). *Literacy in nursery education.* Stoke-on-Trent, UK: Trentham Books.

Campbell, R. (1999). *Literacy from home to school: Reading with Alice.* Stoke-on-Trent, UK: Trentham.

Campbell, R.E. (1998). A day of literacy learning in a nursery classroom. In R. Campbell (Ed.), *Facilitating preschool literacy* (pp. 131–142). Newark, DE: International Reading Association.

Campbell, R., & Scrivens, G. (1995). The teacher role during Sustained Silent Reading. *Reading, 29*(2), 2–4.

Carter, J. (1999). The power and the story. *Reading, 33*(2), 87–90.

Chambers, A. (1995). *Book talk: Occasional writing on literature and children.* Stroud, UK: The Thimble Press.

Chomsky-Higgins, P. (1998). Teaching strategies and skills during readers' workshop: Setting the stage for successful readers and writers. In C. Weaver (Ed.), *Practicing what we know: Informed reading instruction* (pp. 140–153). Urbana, IL: National Council of Teachers of English.

Chukovsky, K. (1963). *From two to five.* Berkeley, CA: University of California Press.

Cullinan, B.E. (1989). Literature for young children. In D.S. Strickland & L.M. Morrow (Eds.), *Emerging literacy: Young children learn to read and write* (pp. 35–51). Newark, DE: International Reading Association.

Cunningham, P.M., & Allington, R.L. (1998). *Classrooms that work: They can all read and write* (2nd ed.). New York: Longman.

Doake, D. (1988). *Reading begins at birth.* Richmond Hill, ON: Scholastic.

Dombey, H. (1988). Partners in the telling. In M. Meek & C. Mills (Eds.), *Language and literacy in the primary school* (pp. 69–81). Lewes, UK: Falmer.

Dunning, D., Mason, J., & Stewart, J. (1994). Reading to preschoolers: A response to Scarborough and Dobrich (1994) and recommendations for the future. *Developmental Review, 14,* 324–339.

Elley, W. (1989). Vocabulary acquisition from listening to stories. *Reading Research Quarterly, 24,* 176–186.

Ericson, L., & Juliebö, M.F. (1998). *The phonological awareness handbook for kindergarten and primary teachers.* Newark, DE: International Reading Association.

Evans, J. (1998, October/November). Perfect circles. *Literacy & Learning,* 16–19.

Feitelson, D., Kita, B., & Goldstein, Z. (1986). Effects of listening to series stories on first graders' comprehension and use of language. *Research in the Teaching of English, 20,* 339–356.

Fountas, I.C., & Pinnell, G.S. (1996). *Guided reading: Good first teaching for all children.* Portsmouth, NH: Heinemann.

Fox, C. (1993). *At the very edge of the forest: The influence of literature on storytelling by children.* London: Cassell.

Geekie, P., Cambourne, B., & Fitzsimmons, P. (1999). *Understanding literacy development.* Stoke-on-Trent, UK: Trentham.

Giorgis, C., & Johnson, N. (1999). Children's books: Reading aloud. *The Reading Teacher, 53,* 80–87.

Goddard, N. (1958). *Reading in the modern infants' school.* London: University of London Press.

Goodman, Y.M. (Ed.). (1990). *How children construct literacy: Piagetian perspectives.* Newark, DE: International Reading Association.

Goodwin, P., & Redfern, A. (2000). *Non-fiction in the literacy hour.* Reading, Berkshire, UK: Reading and Language Information Centre.

Goswami, U. (1999). Causal connections in beginning reading: The importance of rhyme. *Journal of Research in Reading, 22*(3), 217–240.

Goswami, U.C., & Bryant, P. (1990). *Phonological skills and learning to read.* Hove, UK: Erlbaum.

Graham, J., & Kelly, A. (1997). *Reading under control: Teaching reading in the primary school.* London: David Fulton.

Graves, D.H. (1994). *A fresh look at writing.* Portsmouth, NH: Heinemann.

Hall, N., & Robinson, A. (1985). *Looking at literacy: Using images of literacy to explore the world of reading and writing.* London: David Fulton.

Hart-Hewins, L., & Wells, J. (1990). *Real books for reading: Learning to read with children's literature.* Portsmouth, NH: Heinemann.

Hart-Hewins, L., & Wells, J. (1999). *Better books! Better readers.* Markham, ON: Pembroke.

Heath, S.B. (1982). What no bedtime stories means: Narrative skills at home and school. *Language and Society, 11,* 49–76.

Heath, S.B. (1983). *Ways with words: Language, life and work in communities and classrooms.* Cambridge, UK: Cambridge University Press.

Holdaway, D. (1979). *The foundations of literacy.* London: Ashton Scholastic.

Hood, W. (1994). "Did they know he had slaves when they elected him?" Young children can ask powerful questions. In S. Steffey & W. Hood (Eds.), *If this is social studies, why isn't it boring?* (pp. 107–120). York, ME: Stenhouse.

Hoodless, P. (Ed.). (1998). *History and English in the primary school: Exploiting the links.* London: Routledge.

International Reading Association & National Association for the Education of Young Children. (1998). *Learning to read and write: Developmentally appropriate practices for young children.* Newark, DE: International Reading Association; Washington, DC: National Association for the Education of Young Children.

Johnson, P. (1995). *Children making books.* Reading, Berkshire, UK: University of Reading, Reading and Language Information Centre.

Johnson, T., & Louis, D. (1985). *Literacy through literature.* Melbourne, Australia: Thomas Nelson.

Jones, R. (1996). *Emerging patterns of literacy: A multidisciplinary perspective.* London: Routledge.

Kane, S. (1999). Teaching decoding strategies without destroying story. *The Reading Teacher, 52,* 770–772.

Karchmer, R. (2000). Using the Internet and children's literature to support interdisciplinary instruction. *The Reading Teacher, 54,* 100–104.

Kirby, P. (1995). *Successful storysharing for parents and teachers.* Widnes, UK: United Kingdom Reading Association.

Laminack, L. (1991). *Learning with Zachary.* Richmond Hill, ON: Scholastic.

Langer, J.A. (1995). *Envisioning literature: Literary understanding and literature instruction.* New York: Teachers College Press.

Lonigan, C. (1994). Reading to preschoolers exposed: Is the emperor really naked? *Developmental Review, 14,* 303–323.

Marriott, S. (1995). *Read on: Using fiction in the primary school.* London: Paul Chapman.

Martens, P. (1996). *I already know how to read: A child's view of literacy.* Portsmouth, NH: Heinemann.

McCarrier, A., Pinnell, G.S., & Fountas, I.C. (1999). *Interactive writing: How language & literacy come together, K–2.* Portsmouth, NH: Heinemann.

McGee, L.M. (1995). Talking about books with young children. In N.L. Roser & M.G. Martinez (Eds.), *Book talk and beyond: Children and teachers respond to literature* (pp. 105–115). Newark, DE: International Reading Association.

Meek, M. (1988). *How texts teach what readers learn.* Stroud, UK: Thimble Press.

Meek, M. (1990). What do we know about reading that helps us to teach? In R. Carter (Ed.), *Knowledge about language and the curriculum* (pp. 145–153). London: Hodder & Stoughton.

Money, T. (1987). Early literacy. In G. Blenkin & A. Kelly (Eds.), *Early childhood education: A developmental curriculum* (pp. 139–161). London: Paul Chapman.

Mooney, M. (1990). *Reading to, with, and by children.* Katonah, NY: Richard C. Owen.

Morado, C., Koenig, R., & Wilson, A. (1999). Miniperformances, many stars! Playing with stories. *The Reading Teacher, 53,* 116–123.

Morrow, L.M. (1988). Young children's responses to one-to-one story readings in school settings. *Reading Research Quarterly, 23,* 89–107.

Morrow, L.M. (1989). Designing the classroom to promote literacy development. In D.S. Strickland & L.M. Morrow (Eds.), *Emerging literacy: Young children learn to read and write* (pp. 121–134). Newark, DE: International Reading Association.

Morrow, L.M. (1992). The impact of a literature-based program on literacy achievement, use of literature, and attitudes of children from minority backgrounds. *Reading Research Quarterly, 27,* 250–275.

Moustafa, M. (1997). *Beyond traditional phonics: Research discoveries and reading instruction.* Portsmouth, NH: Heinemann.

Neuman, S. (1998). How can we enable all children to achieve? In S.B. Neuman & K.A. Roskos (Eds.), *Children achieving: Best practices in early literacy* (pp. 5–19). Newark, DE: International Reading Association.

Nutbrown, C. (1994). *Threads of thinking: Young children learning and the role of early education.* London: Paul Chapman.

Opie, I., & Opie, P. (1959). *The lore and language of school children.* Oxford, UK: Oxford University Press.

Opitz, M.F. (2000). *Rhymes and reasons: Literature and language play for phonological awareness.* Portsmouth, NH: Heinemann.

Pahl, K. (1999). *Transformations: Children's meaning making in a nursery.* Stoke-on-Trent, UK: Trentham Books.

Phillips, G., & McNaughton, S. (1990). The practice of storybook reading to preschoolers in mainstream New Zealand families. *Reading Research Quarterly, 25,* 196–212.

Phinn, G. (2000). *Young readers and their books: Suggestions and strategies for using texts in the literacy hour.* London: David Fulton.

Powell, D., & Hornsby, D. (1998). Learning phonics while sharing and responding to literature. In C. Weaver (Ed.), *Practicing what we know: Informed reading instruction* (pp. 80–86). Urbana, IL: National Council of Teachers of English.

Rhodes, L. (1981). I can read! Predictable books as resources for reading and writing instruction. *The Reading Teacher, 34,* 511–518.

Rosenblatt, L.M. (1978). *The reader, the text, the poem.* Cambridge, MA: Harvard University Press.

Roser, N.L., & Martinez, M.G. (Eds.). (1995). *Book talk and beyond: Children and teachers respond to literature.* Newark, DE: International Reading Association.

Routman, R. (1991). *Invitations: Changing as teachers and learners K–12.* Portsmouth, NH: Heinemann.

Scarborough, H., & Dobrich, W. (1994). On the efficacy of reading to preschoolers. *Developmental Review, 14,* 245–302.

Schickedanz, J.A. (1990). *Adam's righting revolutions.* Portsmouth, NH: Heinemann.

Short, K. (1999). The search for "balance" in literacy instruction. *English in Education, 33*(3), 43–53.

Slaughter, J.P. (1993). *Beyond storybooks: Young children and shared book experience.* Newark, DE: International Reading Association.

Sloan, G.D. (1991). *The child as critic: Teaching literature in elementary and middle schools* (3rd ed.). New York: Teachers College Press.

Smith, J., & Elley, W. (1994). *Learning to read in New Zealand.* Katonah, NY: Richard C. Owen.

Spreadbury, J. (1994). *Read me a story: Parents, teachers and children as partners in literacy learning.* Carlton, Victoria, Australia: Australian Reading Association.

Strickland, D.S. (1998). *Teaching phonics today: A primer for educators.* Newark, DE: International Reading Association.

Strickland, D.S., & Cullinan, B.E. (1990). Afterword. In M.J. Adams, *Beginning to read: Thinking and learning about print.* Cambridge, MA: MIT Press.

Strickland, D.S., & Morrow, L.M. (1989). Interactive experiences with storybook reading. *The Reading Teacher, 42,* 322–323.

Taylor, D., & Strickland, D.S. (1986). *Family storybook reading.* New York: Scholastic.

Teale, W. (1984). Reading to young children: Its significance for literacy development. In H. Goelman, A. Oberg, & F. Smith (Eds.), *Awakening to literacy* (pp.110–121). London: Heinemann.

Teale, W., & Sulzby, E. (1989). Emergent literacy: New perspectives. In D.S. Strickland & L.M. Morrow (Eds.), *Emerging literacy: Young children learn to read and write* (pp. 1–15). Newark, DE: International Reading Association.

Tizard, B., & Hughes, M. (1984). *Young children learning: Talking and thinking at home and at school*. London: Fontana.

Trelease, J. (1995). *The read-aloud handbook* (4th ed.). New York: Penguin.

Wade, B. (Ed.). (1990). *Reading for real*. Buckingham, UK: Open University Press.

Watson, V. (1993). Multi-layered texts and multi-layered readers. *Cambridge Journal of Education, 23*(1), 15–24.

Weinberger, J., Hannon, P., & Nutbrown, C. (1990). *Ways of working with parents to promote literacy development*. Sheffield, UK: University of Sheffield Division of Education.

Wells, G. (1986). *The meaning makers: Children learning language and using language to learn*. London: Hodder and Stoughton.

White, D. (1984). *Books before five*. Portsmouth, NH: Heinemann. (Original work published 1954)

Whitehead, M. (1987). Narrative, stories and the world of literature. In G. Blenkin & A. Kelly (Eds.), *Early childhood education: A developmental curriculum* (pp. 111–138). London: Paul Chapman.

Children's Literature References

Ahlberg, J., & Ahlberg, A. (1978). *Each peach pear plum*. Harlow, Essex, UK: Oliver & Boyd.

Amery, H. (1989). *Barn on fire*. London: Usborne.

Base, G. (1986). *Animalia*. New York: Harry Abrams.

Burton, V. (1977). *Mike Mulligan and his steam shovel*. Harmondsworth, UK: Puffin Books.

Butterfield, M. (1995). *Zoo animals*. Loughborough, UK: Ladybird.

Carle, E. (1969). *The very hungry caterpillar*. New York: Philomel Books.

Carle, E. (1990). *Pancakes, pancakes*. New York: Simon & Schuster.

Carle, E. (1991). *Do you want to be my friend?* Boston: Houghton Mifflin.

Dodd, L. (1983). *Hairy Maclary from Donaldson's Dairy*. Harmondsworth, UK: Puffin Books.

Dodd, L. (1985a). *Hairy Maclary scattercat*. Harmondsworth, UK: Puffin Books.

Dodd, L. (1985b). *Hairy Maclary's rumpus at the vet*. Harmondsworth, UK: Puffin Books.

Dodd, L. (1993). *Slinky Malinki, open the door*. Harmondsworth, UK: Puffin Books.

Dodd, L. (1995). *Sniff-snuff-snap!* Harmondsworth, UK: Puffin Books.

Dunbar, J. (1991). *Four fierce kittens*. London: Orchard Books.

Fox, M. (1983). *Possum magic*. New York: Harcourt Brace.

Fox, M. (1988). *Koala Lou*. New York: Harcourt Brace.

Fox, M. (1995). *Wombat Divine*. Sydney, Australia: Scholastic Australia Group.

Hutchins, P. (1972). *Good-night owl*. London: The Bodley Head.

Hutchins, P. (1987). *Rosie's walk*. New York: Scholastic.

Lacome, J. (1993). *Walking through the jungle*. London: Walker Books.

Lenski, L. (1946). *The little train*. Oxford, UK: Oxford University Press.

Oxenbury, H. (1993). *It's my birthday*. London: Walker Books.

Radcliffe, T. (1997). *Cimru the seal*. Harmondsworth, UK: Puffin Books.

Seuss, Dr. (1960). *Green eggs and ham*. New York: Random House.

Seuss, Dr. (1963). *Hop on Pop*. New York: Random House.

Waddell, M. (1988). *Can't you sleep, little bear?* London: Walker Books.

Waddell, M. (1991). *Let's go home, little bear*. Cambridge, MA: Candlewick Press.

Wadsworth, G. (1999). *One tiger growls*. Watertown, MA: Charlesbridge.

Walsh, J. (1997). *When I was little like you*. Harmondsworth, UK: Puffin Books.

Wilhelm, H. (1985). *I'll always love you*. London: Hodder.

Index